The Road to
Key West Ink

The Road to Key West Ink

*A Road Shadowed
by Greed and Deceit*

By "Boe" Mencarelli

As told to Rosemary Hoffman-Murray

To order additional copies of this book, contact:
Xlibris Corporation
1-888-795-4274
www.Xlibris.com
Orders@Xlibris.com
57309

This book is dedicated to all of the "little guys" who are trying to open and run a small business or who have successfully done so. I want to thank my wife, Patty for her support. I also want to thank my crew at Tat2Times Inc. for bearing with me as I race back and forth between Key West and Palm Bay to make my dream a reality. I also want to thank Rosemary Hoffman-Murray for her help in writing and editing this book.

Introduction

This is the story of my love affair with the art of tattooing. How can tattoo be termed an art you might ask? Well, in my world and in the world of tattoo artists all over the world, art is a beautiful creation that is not necessarily created with oil paint or watercolors or clay. Tattoos are *skin* art that often tell a story about the person who has chosen to have one inscribed on him or her.

Be it a small rendering on one part of the body (say, a rose on the shoulder or a butterfly on a thigh), or a complete story or fantasy mixed with reality that covers whole areas of skin, tattoo art is an outlet for a lot of folks who would otherwise never consider art that appears on canvas or is made by talented hands.

Tattoo art chose me rather than the other way around. I got started shortly after leaving the service in the early 1980's. Living in San Francisco, I was given the opportunity to use ink as my color palette and many willing folks gave up their skin . . . their canvas, so to speak . . . so that I could paint their own personal story for the whole world to see.

My life has been one of great ups and downs; sadness, adventure, love, laughter and fulfillment. I hope that you enjoy my short tale of how I came to be the professional artist that I am today and how important it is to me to open the minds and eyes of Key West Florida's citizens to what tattoo art is and what it is not.

My adventure has not ended with this book. I am still fighting to get back what is rightfully mine from a partner who used my talents to get his foot in the door of an arena that was previously closed to him and to all tattoo artists in this crazy, funky little city where almost anything goes (literally). I am fighting fair, as I do not relish back biting tactics when it comes to getting what is rightfully mine. This fight is still going on today, even as you read this book, and you will understand more about what I am talking about once you get into my story.

The Road to Key West Ink is my personal tale of a dream fulfilled . . . and then abruptly taken away. And I plan to realize that dream once again.

Thanks for reading.

Boe Mencarelli

I

In the summer of 2006, I sat outside my studio, Tat2Times Inc. in Palm Bay, Florida and watched as a huge black Hummer pulled into the parking lot. Two people climbed out, a heavy set middle aged man and a woman a little bit younger, with graying blonde hair. She was smoking a cigarette and both were smiling as they approached me. Right away, I noticed that neither of them had tattoos, at least from what I could see. The man had a Hemingway type beard and wore an Australian bush hat with flaps that were pinned up on the sides and a chin strap he had slung to the back of his head, resting on a six inch pony tail. The man seemed to know who I was and shook my hand aggressively.

His name was John and he was quick to make small talk. He told me he was a contractor by trade specializing in stucco. His business was located south of Brevard County, in Vero Beach. The woman didn't say anything as John continued to tell me about his business, how much money he made and how successful he was. I guessed by the size and type of vehicle he drove that he was pretty well off but I wondered why he was telling me all of this. I quickly cut him off and asked what I could do for him. He wanted to take a look around my shop, see what kind of operation I ran, and maybe have some skin art done. I held the door for both of them as they walked into my studio where two of my other artists were busy with customers.

As they looked around my shop, they appeared impressed not only by the photographs of my work but by the awards and write ups I had received. He asked about the photographs hanging on the wall along with the standard tattoo pictures that were displayed to give people ideas for their own art work. We talked some about various types of tattoos, the process of time it takes to do various jobs and so on.

Now this man did not have a drop of ink on him and suddenly he told me he wanted both of his arms done . . . full "sleeves" as we call it in this business . . . and possibly his entire back inked as well. I had to smile. I figured him to be about forty-nine or fifty and perhaps he was going through a midlife crisis or something. The Hummer outside appeared new, it was probably an impulse buy. And it's not every day that a guy just walks into my shop and tells me he wants that much work done, particularly if he has never had a tattoo in his life. I also wondered why he had chosen my shop from the array of studios in and around Brevard County but figured he was just impressed with my awards and the write ups that had been done about my work. John and his wife, Tammy browsed through my portfolio and he became excited about various photos and pictures that I showed them. He asked a dozen or more questions about the process and seemed really interested when I showed him a five page spread in a European based tattoo magazine that featured my art.

"Wow, this is pretty impressive!" he commented. "You are definitely my man," I wasn't sure if I should consider that a compliment or not.

John became very comfortable with me as an artist, realizing that I did, indeed, know what I was doing. He decided right there and then that he wanted to get the work done and he wanted to begin right away. There were no other customers in the shop, and I wasn't expecting any for the next few hours, so I made him comfortable and we got to work.

My studio is divided up into cubicles so that each customer has complete privacy while they have the art work done. The chairs are extremely comfortable and I have had people sit for hours during one session without complaining. I also keep my shop super clean because I have seen too many dirty studios where it is obvious the owner doesn't care whether or not someone walks out with a disease or an infection. My reputation is one I am extremely proud of and I would never do anything to ruin that.

I picked his brain a little to feel out what direction he wanted to go with the art, the theme and the look of the sleeves when they were complete. Like a lot of people who come into the studio for tattoos, he really had no idea of what he wanted. It would be up to me to pull information from him so that I could get an idea of what I was working with. We talked some more and I was able to acquire some inspirations based on his life and what was important to him. With tattoos, (and in particular, full sleeves), most people want to have art created that represents significant people, places or things in their individual lives or personalities. And for John, this meant pirates.

Don't ask me why . . . but he was stuck like glue on the pirate theme. Eventually, he landed on a theme of a pirate and a scroll with the words "Stucco Man" on it. He spent several hours in my chair that first day, coming up with more ideas and recounting various occurrences in his life. I concentrated on the art work and let him talk, figuring he was most comfortable that way. The pirate I had created was quite large, which is what he wanted, and ornate. He liked the colors I had used and was more than happy when it was done. He was smiling ear to ear like a little boy with a bag of candy . . . in this case, "skin candy". He and his wife, who had been watching the whole process closely, left for the day and I knew he would be coming back for more work soon.

John visited the shop again two weeks later. He sat for five hours of work, talking my ear off the whole time. He told me he had been going to Key West for the past few years and that he had finally purchased a house there. Ah, so that was the reason for the pirate theme! Key West flaunts pirate attire and attitude at every corner.

He cleared his throat and watched as I worked, still staying completely still.

"You know, Boe, there hasn't been a tattoo shop in Key West for nearly forty years. What do you think about that?" he said.

I was a little surprised. Key West is known to be one of the most liberal cities in the U.S., flaunting its Gay scene, nude bars, burlesque shows and folks drinking cocktails as they shopped the gaudy tee-shirt stores and upscale jewelry and apparel shops. It is a crazy and fun place and it seemed only natural that a tattoo parlor would adorn the main drag, Duval Street.

"That's strange" I commented as I worked on his skin. "Why is that?"

John said he didn't know but he would find out. At that time, I wondered why he would be interested in something like this. He didn't seem interested in becoming a skin artist himself that was for sure. I had the distinct feeling he had something on his mind and maybe he was getting the tattoos done so he could learn the process himself. However, I knew that learning to create a tattoo was an art, not something anyone could just pick up because he or she wanted to. There are plenty of ink slingers out there who haven't got a clue as to what they are doing and most of them don't last in the business very long. So if that was what he had in mind, I knew he would be in over his head. My own artists are all professionals and have either been schooled in fine art or have a natural talent. Their portfolios are large and show high quality work done on various customers as well as other art mediums they might specialize in, such as oil or water color painting.

I kept my mouth shut, though. He was turning out to be a profitable customer and someone I genuinely liked. I could tell he was full of bull a lot of the time, but that was okay, he was interesting and sure as hell I did not want to shoot down any far flung ideas he may have had regarding joining the tattoo industry. He could daydream all he liked as far as I was concerned. I just wanted to concentrate on my work and do a great job for him. I knew he would be a great "walking advertisement" for my work when we were all done.

It took five hours to work the pigment into his skin to create the image he wanted. It was amazing how he could just sit there, like a rock. Some of my crew even started calling him "The Rock". Later on, as the work progressed on John to include his back, he started talking about Key West again and I knew the guy had a motive for getting all of this ink done. Sure, he was getting great custom work at decent prices, but I knew now that there was something else going on in his head. He was coming into the shop week after week, sometimes for eight hours at a time, sitting just as still as always but running his mouth, telling me all kinds of things about his life and then always bringing up Key West again.

"It's a wild scene," he told me one time. "You oughta' get down there sometime."

I laughed. I explained to him that I had a studio up in Washington State in Olympia and I barely had time to get up there much less take a trip down to the Keys even for a day or two. It was grinding on me because I couldn't get up there much, I was so busy here in Florida. But the studio up there was profitable when I was manning it. When I was away, however, it seemed the place would go all to hell.

"The crew I have up there just doesn't seem to understand that a tattoo place needs to be kept clean," I told him. "The floor gets dirty, dust is everywhere. It can be a real mess. One time, I took a trip up there and found some of my guys smoking weed and young girls . . . girls not old enough to get tattoos let alone smoke dope . . . floating around like stoned groupies inside the shop. I finally had to show my guys how to strip and wax the floor, kind of a "hands on demo with a practical application". Of course, the demo part didn't work because every time I showed up there, the place was filthy again."

John smiled. "Sounds like you really know what needs to be done to keep a business going. Sure is hard to get good help sometimes though, huh? I know all about that."

I told him I really couldn't complain too much. The Washington studio was good to me all in all. When I spent time there, we made a lot of money and the locals were really happy with the work we did. But I was spending more and more time in Florida and I was wondering if it was time to sell it off and just maintain my business in Palm Bay.

I explained this all to John, who didn't look too interested, he just kept talking about Key West. We were almost done with the work he wanted on his arms and back and it had been almost a year since we had started on him. That's when his wife decided to jump on the ink wagon, wanting to get a tattoo of her own. She chose a dragon fly hovering over a two-strand length of barbed wire that appeared to fade into her skin as it came around each side. Later, she would want the barbed wire theme around the front of her body and there would be roses laced throughout the wire, with stems from the roses heading south on her body.

John was hanging around the shop one day, watching me work on Tammy, when he brought Key West up again. He had finally got the skinny on what was going on there as far as tattoo operations were concerned. It turned out that the city had placed a ban on tattooing back in the early 60's primarily due to a Navy ordinance. The tattoo studios in place at that time were operating in less than a sterile environment. The Navy commander at the time did not want his troops going downtown, getting drunk and risking disease or infection from what they considered to be a "seedy environment." So the Navy asked the city to do something about it. In other words, the Navy said "You either shut down the tattoo studios or the downtown area will be off limits for all Navy personnel." Back in the sixties, the city of Key west isn't what it is today. The city depended a great deal on the Navy as a source of revenue, and if the Navy made the downtown area off limits to its personnel, it would put a great strain on the local economy. And so it was, in 1964 the city placed in effect an ordinance banning all tattooing inside the city limits. The nearest tattoo studios were on Stock Island, a couple of miles north of Key West. The tourists did not know about these places and if they did, they weren't inclined to make the short trip over there to have any work done. A lot of tattoo art is a spur of the moment thing . . . people see the art in a storefront window and decide then and there they want some work done. Whether it is a small tattoo on one area of the body or a full sleeve or two, a lot of folks choose to have work done on impulse."I think," John told me as he watched me work on Tammy, "that Key West could use a place like this. Something with class, maybe on Duval Street, right in the heart of the city. The problem is, we'd have to get the city to okay it. That could be a bitch."

We? I thought. *Was he talking about him and me?* I now knew what he had been leading up to all along.

"What do you think Boe?" He asked excitedly.

I stopped what I was doing and looked over at him.

"About what?" I asked.

"About you and me trying something like this? Opening a studio in Key West?"

I thought about it for a minute or two, no longer, and grinned. "You serious man?"

He nodded and I grinned.

"Sure, what the hell?" I said. "Let's do it!"

So that was the beginning of the craziest adventure of my life. But "Crazy" is my middle name and I knew it would come as no surprise when I told my wife Patty about it.

II

When I was a kid, I bounced from foster home to foster home, each one worse than the other. With me was my twin brother, Walter. It seemed we were in a different home every month. These were group homes containing up to a dozen kids, and we often got lost in the shuffle, as did the others. To most group home families, we represented dollars and cents, money in their pockets for taking care of us. If you can call it that. Foster parents receive a check for every child they had in their care and it is still the same way today. In group homes, where there were many kids from different families, that money could mean up to 5000.00 or so a month. That's a lot of cash to some people and often, group home parents were not very well off. They really counted on this money to make ends meet and so it was that they agreed to take in more and more children as income boosters.

There are people out there making a living by housing these foster kids. They don't work outside the home, fostering is their full time job. I remember being in one home where my brother and I were hanging out in the kitchen, just being kids, and I was reaching over the stove for something to eat. I stood up on a chair and reached over the stove where the burner was lit. While reaching for some cookies or something, my skinny little belly came to rest on the lit burner and I received a terrible burn on my bare skin. I still have the scar today. But it is not nearly as bad as the scar caused by my so-called foster "mother" who came running in, screaming at the top of her lungs.

"What are you brats doing! You know you're not supposed to be in here!" she yelled. She was not worried about me burning myself; she was pissed off because I had done such a stupid thing. She lashed out not just at me, but at my brother as well. For some reason, she grabbed his hands and slammed them down on the still-lit burners, scorching his skin, and I can still hear him screaming in pain and terror to this day.

"That'll teach you brats to take things that don't belong to you!" she yelled. She slammed the kitchen door as she left us there, crying and screaming. There was no medical attention offered to either of us and we both wear the ugly scars of that day even now.

Soon, we found ourselves in yet another group home. The "parents" of this home were hard drinkers and liked to party a lot. One night, they were having some sort of shindig and the kids were relegated to their bedrooms to be kept quiet and out of sight. My brother and I decided to have our own party. We played a game we called "Circus".

Our beds were on the opposite sides of the room, which was very small, and they were maybe four or five feet apart at the most. We started to bounce back and fourth from one bed to the other, giggling and carrying on as kids do. This was such fun and it is a wonder neither of us fell onto the floor and cracked our tail bones or our heads. Eventually, we heard the door to our room open and our newest "mother" came rushing in, screaming and swinging a belt like it was some kind of Samurai sword.

"What the hell do you kids think you are doing?" she screamed, waving the belt drunkenly in front of us. Her face was twisted in a look of sheer hatred and I took a couple of mean lashes before I was able to retreat under my bed. She then went for Walter with rage in her eyes. She was yelling something that only a fellow drunk would understand, we certainly didn't have a clue as to why she was so mad. From the sound my brother made as he was hit with the belt, I knew she was really hurting him.

What happened next will stay with me my entire life and I still remember it as if it were only yesterday: My brother, while trying to get away from this evil belt-swinging madwoman, caught the buckle of the belt right in the eye. He screamed bloody murder and tried to scuttle under his bed as she kept lashing at him.

Finally, she stopped hitting him and yelled into the room that the two of us better get into our beds and go to sleep or there would be "hell to pay".

We thought it had already been paid. We were crying and shaking, as scared as rabbits hiding from hunters in the woods. I will never forget the look on my brother's face, the swollen blood spot of his eye, the tears raining down his cheeks.

The next morning, my brother was finally taken to the local hospital. But it was too late; he had already lost sight in that eye. Our foster mother was not charged, of course, because she made up some story about how he had fallen on a toy in our bedroom and we weren't about to tell the truth . . . that would mean more torture from this mad woman and possibly from her husband. So we kept quiet, and let them cover Walter's eye with a patch and listened as the Doctor told her he was so "sorry" that this had happened.

Some years later, Walter would be forced to have his eye removed due to glaucoma that was caused, indirectly, by that injury to his eye when he was just a kid. If they had not removed his eye, the glaucoma might migrate to the other eye and he would be blind. It was this loss to his eye that kept my brother from participating in sports or any organized team activities which I excelled in and he, more than likely, would have excelled in also.

Eventually, Walter and I were adopted by a kind and generous family when we were six years old. My mother's name was Carolina but most people called her Kay. My father was Carlo, but for some reason, folks called him Charlie. We lived in a brown split level ranch home in Boston. I remember that spring was right around the corner when we arrived at our new home and our parents had bought us these cool little white outfits complete with new socks and shoes to wear home so they could show us off to the neighbors and other family members. Well, there was a huge field down the road that had everything a sports nut, or in our case, a couple of wild and crazy kids, could ever want: Three baseball fields, four basket ball courts, tennis courts and a soccer field transformed into a football field during football season. Within minutes, the two of us had found our way down the muddy path to these sports arenas and found ourselves in mud puddles a foot or so deep. Oh, boy, I thought. We are gonna' be in big trouble now! Of course, we were so used to getting into trouble with our foster parents, we just assumed that our new "real" parents would be angry that we had messed up our brand new clothes and would tear us up one side and down the other.

Well, as luck had it, our new mom came running down to retrieve us and did not even flinch when she saw us. In fact, she acted apologetic that we had wandered off on our own and she gently took our hands and walked us back up to the house. Walter and I both knew, at that point, that we had found ourselves a real home.

That playground would become a second home for us while we grew up in the Kay and Charlie Mencarelli home. Mencarelli is indeed an Italian name as dad came over to this country by himself from Italy when he was just a young teenager. He had no relatives in America and I can only imagine what he must have gone through when he arrived in New York City back in 1929 at such a very young age. He was born in Naples, Italy in 1913 and he was the first in his family to migrate to the United States. He worked in labor for many years in the States, but went home to Italy when war broke out. He found himself lugging a machine gun through most of the war and received several medals for courage under fire. He was hit several times and one of his wounds would even earn him a ticket home. Back in the States after the war, he continued to work as a laborer, but what he really wanted to do was masonry work, or rather, field stone work. Eventually, he was one of the most sought after field stone masons around. There wasn't much he couldn't do with field stone and bricks. At a young age, I found myself helping him with a project he had started. His idea was to build a stone wall that went around our property. The wall was made of field stones that we would gather from deep in the woods in the New England area. Apparently, borders of stone walls once separated properties hundreds of years ago. As they wore down, they became a field stone mason's dream, perfect for use on large areas of land as wall dividers.

It took almost three years to finish that wall to dad's satisfaction. He was a perfectionist when it came to his work and it rubbed off on me. I am that way with the art I create each and every day, from the smallest to the largest of tattoos. He was a fine man with a heart of gold, even if he was a little strict with my brother and me. He taught me the benefits of hard work, a lesson I will never forget. And I hope I have passed this down to my own kids. Mom Kay was super protective over Walter. She wouldn't allow him to do anything that would risk his one good eye. She meant well but sometimes, I think she went a little overboard with the protection she gave him. I was able to play most sports . . . little league and hockey were my two favorites . . . while Walter was relegated to the sidelines. When the sun was shining and school was out, you could often find me practicing ball in the field. When winter came, the field would ice over and I had the best place in town to play hockey. From the time the sun came up until dusk, you'd find me playing hockey, honing my craft so that maybe one day I could be another Buddy Orr or Phil Esposito. And in the summer, I'd be playing ball, hoping to catch up to my heroes Yaz (Carl Yastrzemski) and Ricco Petroselli or Carlton Fisk, all big leaguers with a name for themselves.

School was never my favorite thing. I never really liked it and the only way I got through it was because my mom and dad were damned sure I was going to graduate. During the school year, my day ended at sundown. I wasn't allowed to hang out with my buddies in the neighborhood. Homework always came first, even before I could go outside when it was still daylight. Chores came second . . . chores like cleaning bricks or lugging wood for our pot belly stove that was in our basement of the New England home we lived in. Mom did not give us any slack when it came to getting our chores done and the value of hard work was further ingrained in my soul.

Later on, in high school, I was the kid who would sit in the back of the classroom doodling drawings in my notebook, not paying attention to the teacher. I loved to draw and thought one day I would be a cartoonist or an artist of some sort. I was good at it too, even the teachers admitted that much! However, I had to buckle down and hit the books in order to graduate. I actually graduated a little earlier than my other classmates. During my junior year I doubled up on my academic classes so that by senior year, I would only have to stay in school half the year. My principal at the time, Mr. Rice, agreed to cut me loose the day I turned eighteen. I convinced him to do this because I wanted to enlist in the U.S. Army, which I did. Being military minded himself, Mr. Rice was proud to know a kid who was so hopped up about joining the service. I would receive my diploma in the late spring, just like everyone else in my class, only mine would be sent to me via mail.

My folks were not too happy about this at first, but eventually my dad admitted how proud he was of his son, the serviceman. Mom complained that she wanted to see her sons graduate from high school together. Eventually, she got over that, knowing that nothing she said would change my mind.

I enrolled in the delayed entry program so when March 22, 1975 came around, I was on my way to Fort Benning, Georgia. When my class was graduating in June, I was jumping out of a plane. My diploma was mailed to me, and along with it came a document that told me that I had been awarded a scholarship in art. However, because I was in the service, they had given it to someone else.

I sometimes think about how different my life might have been if I hadn't joined the service. But I believe we make the choices we do according to what is in store for your future. Fate, you might say.

Fate or serendipity. Often, they go hand in hand.

III

John and I seemed to be getting along well, becoming pretty good friends. He invited my wife, Patty, and me down to the Keys for a weekend of deep sea fishing. He had recently purchased a new fishing boat and was anxious to show it off. I had never been to the Keys and was anxious to see what all the fuss was about. I knew enough about Key West to expect some craziness going on there, but that was about all. Little did I realize how perfectly beautiful the chain of islands are that make up the whole of the Florida Keys.

Patty and I jumped in the truck, suitcases piled in the back, and took off for this much needed mini vacation of sorts. Driving south, we put on some Jimmy Buffett and Bob Marley to get ourselves in the right frame of mind. We were as excited as two school kids going on a field trip. We drove south on I-95 from Palm Bay and then took the turnpike through Miami into Homestead. From Homestead, we headed south on Route One, where we were overwhelmed with the beauty we encountered. The water on both the gulf side on the West and the Atlantic Ocean on the east were a color of turquoise I had never seen before. The sun glittered like diamonds, bouncing off the surface of both bodies of water. Fishing boats, sail boats and everything in between seemed to be out on the water that day. I can't describe how suddenly relaxed I felt, and this feeling would be one I would encounter every single time I drove into Key Largo, the first major Key of the group.

There are over 800 islands in the Florida Keys. Most are wildlife sanctuaries, uninhabited by human life. The inhabited keys are linked by 42 bridges scattered along the 126 mile historic U.S. route 1, including the fantastic 7-mile bridge. One thing I noticed immediately was that there were mile markers that told you how far you had come and how much farther you had to go. Mile Marker "0" is a historic landmark marking the southernmost point in the United States. There is a giant, colorful buoy marking the spot which is a mere ninety miles away from Cuba. It has been the site of many souvenir photos and of course, we would have to strike a pose for posterity.

As the mile markers got lower, our excitement grew. We would be staying in John and Tammy's house in Key West which he had described as his own paradise on the island. When we got there, we were greeted like family and as soon as we brought our bags in, John suggested we go for a tour of the island . . . via bicycles.

Getting around the island on bikes took a little getting used to. There were cars, motorcycles, big and small trucks, buses, scooters . . . you name it. The bigger vehicles did not have a lot of patience for people . . . particularly tourists . . .

who chose to ride two wheeled bikes in and out of traffic. The roads in Key West are narrow, to say the least, with cars parked at the curbs of shops and restaurants. So it was tricky at first. Once we got the hang of it though, we relaxed and had a great time taking in all the sites.

John and Tammy treated us to a tour of the old neighborhoods where wooden houses were painted various shades of pink, green and lavender. Bahama shutters adorned most of these homes, helping to keep them dry when storm whipped rains and winds visited the town, usually in the summer months. We rode through the downtown streets, stopping for lunch on Duval Street, the main drag in the city. We took in Mallory Square at sunset, watching all the craziness that goes on there when the sun is sinking over the water. Magicians, Mimes, Fire Eaters, Fortune Tellers, Singers, and Dancers, whatever sort of entertainment one could cook up . . . was available on Mallory Square. There were also plenty of shops selling everything from Key Lime Pie to seashells and souvenir postcards. Out to sea, set against the setting sun, were sail boats and large yachts. Everyone was celebrating the Sunset. It is tradition in the Keys to toast the setting sun with drinks and more drinks. Patty and I realized that this was, indeed, one fun and crazy town! We were having a ball.

Eventually, we headed for the town's drinking establishments, many of them on Duval Street. There was Rick's, Sloppy Joe's, Irish Kevin's, Two Friends and then there was a place that blew my mind completely . . . The Garden of Eden. It sits atop the Bull and Whistle pub. Now let me tell you, we were not prepared for what we saw there. The first thing that I noticed as we entered the club was a sign stating that no cameras are allowed inside. Hmmm . . . that seemed odd. The next thing that came to mind when we climbed the steps to the third floor was why in hell would John bring Patty and me (and his wife, Tammy) to a place where there was more bare skin showing then there was booze! But then I thought "Wow! You can get naked in an open air third level bar ;You can drive mopeds in and out of narrow little streets as if you were in the Daytona 500; You can walk around with a drink in each hand as you shop or bar hop; *But you can't get a damned tattoo anywhere inside the city limits of Key West!!"* This made absolutely no sense to me. When I asked John about it, he grinned and shrugged.

"The town godfathers think tattoos are "sleazy"," he said. "Go figure. That's something you and I have to work on, buddy."

After a long weekend of eating and drinking and fishing and taking in all the sights and sounds that Key West had to offer, it was time to head back north to Palm Bay, back to the real world. I had to get ready for another of my many trips to Olympia, Washington. I would be gone for five days this time, but John scheduled another appointment with me for the following week. He had done a lot of research regarding the Keys' restrictions on tattoo studios in their city and so had I. We needed to discuss exactly what it was he had in mind. I pretty much knew he wanted me to do some art for him, but I did not know that I would become so involved in the venture. That was something I would find out, sooner than later.

My trip to Olympia was pretty uneventful, as trips go. I was getting pretty fed up with the way the place was being kept up . . . or rather, *not* being kept up . . . when I wasn't there to supervise operations. I had always been proud of this studio, a two level space with a huge multi paned beveled window on the second floor where the afternoon sun would shine through, creating a natural light to work by. When the sun went down, the view from my parking space was like no other. You could see everything. I had put a lot of work into this place and I hated to see it going down hill. The custom layout was a tattoo artist's dream. It had high ceilings creating a wide open feeling. Indeed, the whole building was created with the artist in mind, an unusual concept. I worked on the intricate staircase myself in a warehouse some thirty miles away that was normally used to build the swift boats used by the coast guard, police and sheriff departments throughout the country. The stairs were made in three separate sections and hauled in via flat bed. At first, we weren't at all sure if they would fit in our studio, even though we had measured carefully throughout the building process. However, it fit like a glove, much to our relief. (Here I have to pause to thank Lonnie and Anthony for their commitment to this project, for it would never have been completed without them). At one time, I also had a small studio in Sacramento California. The area was a little on the seedy side to say the least. The locals referred to it as the D.P.H. . . . the Deepest Part of Hell. Criminal activity was abundant in this part of town, which was just a few blocks away from the bustling business area of the town itself. Seems to me that most large cities are like this . . . they have a thriving business and residential area just a few minutes outside a major criminal Mecca. How the two operate so well together is beyond me.

Anyway, I witnessed a lot of criminal activity when I got out of the service in the summer of 1983. My last duty station was over on the Presidio of San Francisco. Thousands of tourists flock to this city every year for various reasons. The weather is perpetually temperate, the Golden Gate Bridge beckons, and there are tons of restaurants and ethnic areas to explore. There's the ocean, the bay, and Fisherman's Wharf. The street cars and Trolley cars add a lot of flavor. It is just a great town full of history and lots of funky activities for young and old alike.

As a civilian in San Francisco, I mulled over what I wanted to do for a living. I liked the town and the people and figured I would stay on for awhile. I started tending bar in the "tenderloin" area of the city which is well known for its crime and drug scene. The bar where I worked was once owned by the retired chief of Police, believe it or not. It was that bar where I slung a good majority of ink on the side and it was there that I was introduced to a number of the Red and White (Hell's Angels) club members. Little did I know what an effect they would have on my life in California.

The restaurant and bar I worked in, El Picanti, was owned by Steve and Merrissa, a husband and wife team. They were great people. He was Irish American and she was Spanish. They were a great couple, good people. After one particularly long day, Steve was coming up the stairs with some cases of beer and waiting at the top was a disgruntled customer. Surly and drunk, he stood on the top step with a 357 in his right hand and in slurred speech, proceeded to tell Steve that he had kidnapped Merrissa and had her in a motel room just a couple of blocks away. Steve dropped the cases of beer and the drunk unloaded the 357 into Steve's chest. Had I been there, it probably would have been me climbing those stairs with the cases. Maybe it would have been me who would have been shot, or maybe I would have been able to save Steve's life. Whichever, fate played a role that horrible night, that is for sure.

After that night, the drunk was thrown into the slammer where he belonged and Merrissa decided to sell the place. I certainly could not blame her for that. The folks who bought it kept me on. After bartending all day, I was able to sling ink after hours in the bar where I had set up a tattoo station in one corner. I even named my tiny studio "Some Place Else" so people could distinguish it from the bar.

I had begun with what was called a "start up" kit which I got in the military. I upgraded my sterilizer and ultra sonic cleaner, but other than that, I had everything I needed in that kit. There were guys who laughed and said that there was no way I could make a living doing tattoo art and there is one thing you don't want to do and that is to tell me I can't do something . . . then I will become hell on wheels, proving you wrong.

While in San Francisco, I had gone around knocking on doors, trying to get my foot in the door at various tattoo parlors. People looked at me as if I had two heads. I don't know whether it was because of my age (I was 27 at the time) or because I didn't know anyone in this close knit community. I am thinking that maybe it was a little of both. Anyway, I wasn't going to let a couple of slammed doors stop me from what I wanted to do. I am not sure it is something I wanted as far as a career goes; but I did know I wanted to learn more about the art and the finer points of tattooing. But I had to find someone to teach me. The tattoo industry was a close knit community back in those days and the old timers really didn't want to teach the new guys anything about the art. I really needed to get my ass in a shop where I could soak up some of the tricks of the trade, which are abundant in this field. So working until the early morning hours in the heart of the tenderloin district, I began to concentrate on putting together a portfolio of sorts, one that was worth taking a look at. I did a lot more drawing at this time and eventually had a greeting card company approach me about a line of cards I had designed. I didn't take them up on it because I really wanted to make a go at my tattoo business. I knew that if I kept my nose to the grindstone, it would happen for me.

I stayed in San Francisco, working in my little make-shift tattoo studio for almost five years and then headed to Sacramento. There I got my first position in a real shop. The place was called "Above All Tattooing" and I worked there for about eight months, just long enough to absorb what I needed to know and believe me, I took complete advantage of that education. Special techniques, pigmentation mixtures and everything in between became my schoolwork and I think it paid off well.

So after leaving that shop, I decided to open my own place, again called "Some Place Else". I had a business partner that was causing me a lot of hassles, spending the profits from the business on drugs among other things. I put up with it for two years before I packed up my stuff and took off. I didn't want any part of the drug scene, it just wasn't worth it. So just like that, I left that life behind. There is no honor in doing time for another man, and I was tired of putting myself in that spot. I wanted a different life, a good life, one I could call mine. So I headed for Seattle where I heard business was brisk in the tattooing industry and I had always wanted to see that part of the country. I figured the weather would be a lot like that in San Francisco, cool and rainy with some sunshiny days in the summer. That appealed to me.

As I made my way toward Washington State, I had in my mind that I wanted to open a unique, exclusive skin art studio where I would be in control, not sharing control with anyone else. I had found out the hard way that often, a partnership can turn sour when one or the other goes the wrong way, spends money he or she shouldn't. It just plugs up your creative talents, and I wanted to become a *well known* artist, not just another ink slinger working for the man. This time, I knew what I wanted and the basics about how to get it.

It would just take a little time. That's all.

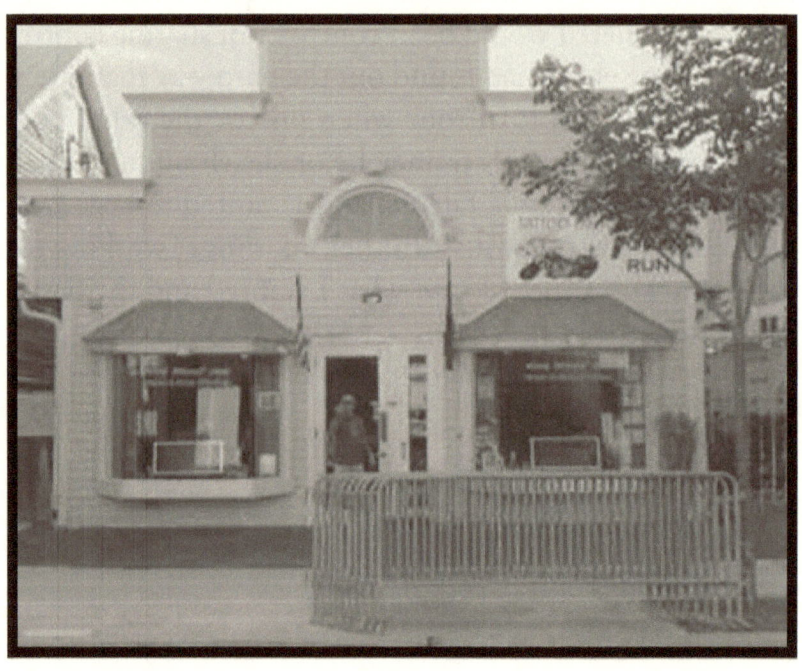

Key West Ink. Oct-08 over a year, and 300.000.00 in profit you would think John could afford a sign and a paint job of the store front. First two rules of business—1. location 2. presentation

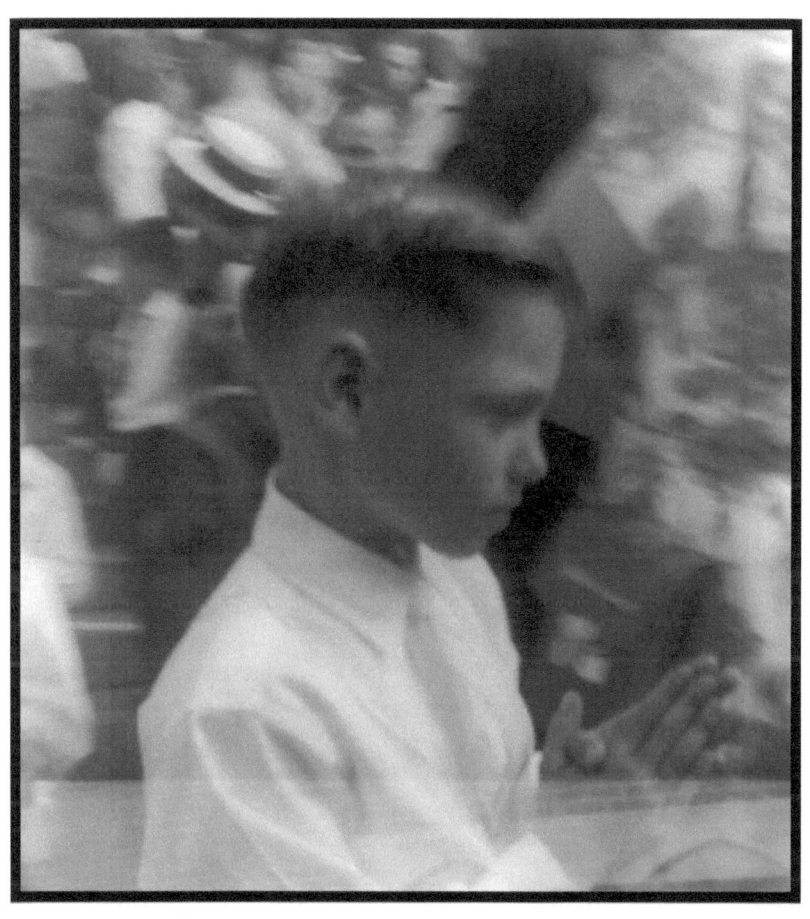

Me @ my first communion

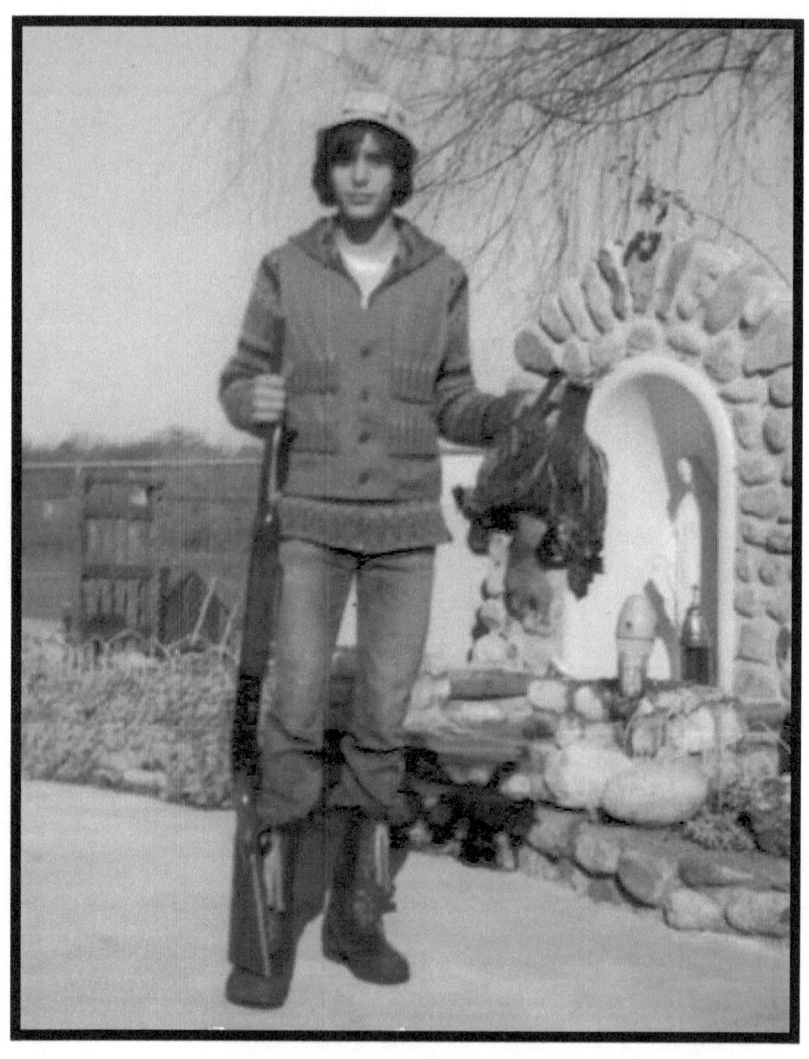

Me after a hunting trip December 1973

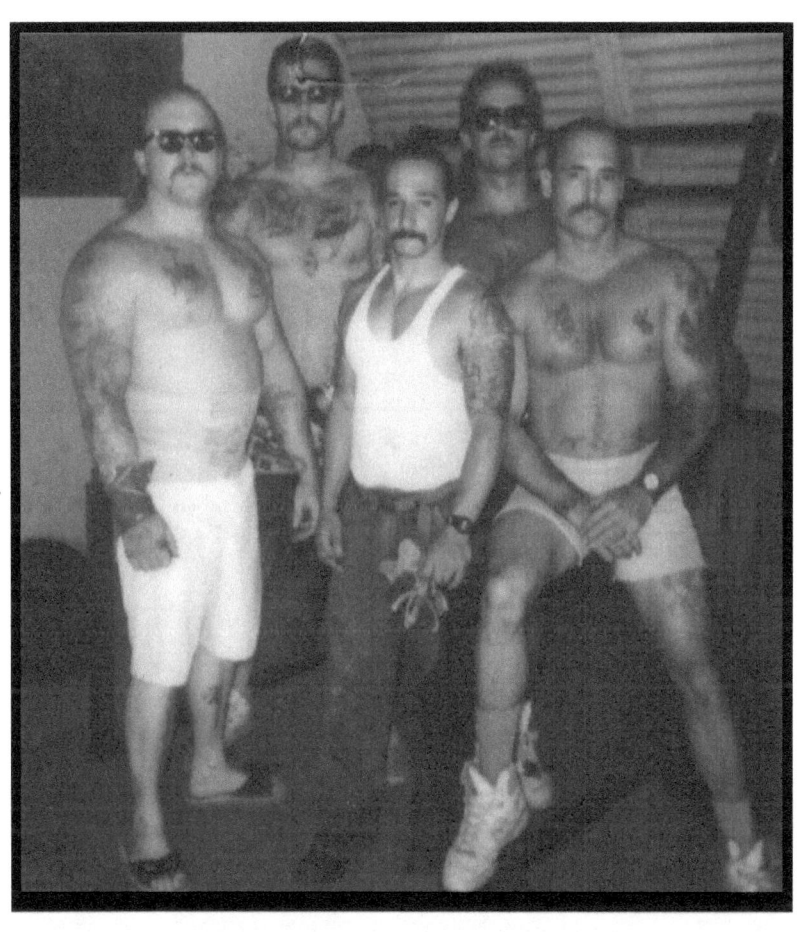

From left to right: Jeff, Anthony, lizard Tim. and I
@ the club house getting our drive on (late 80's)

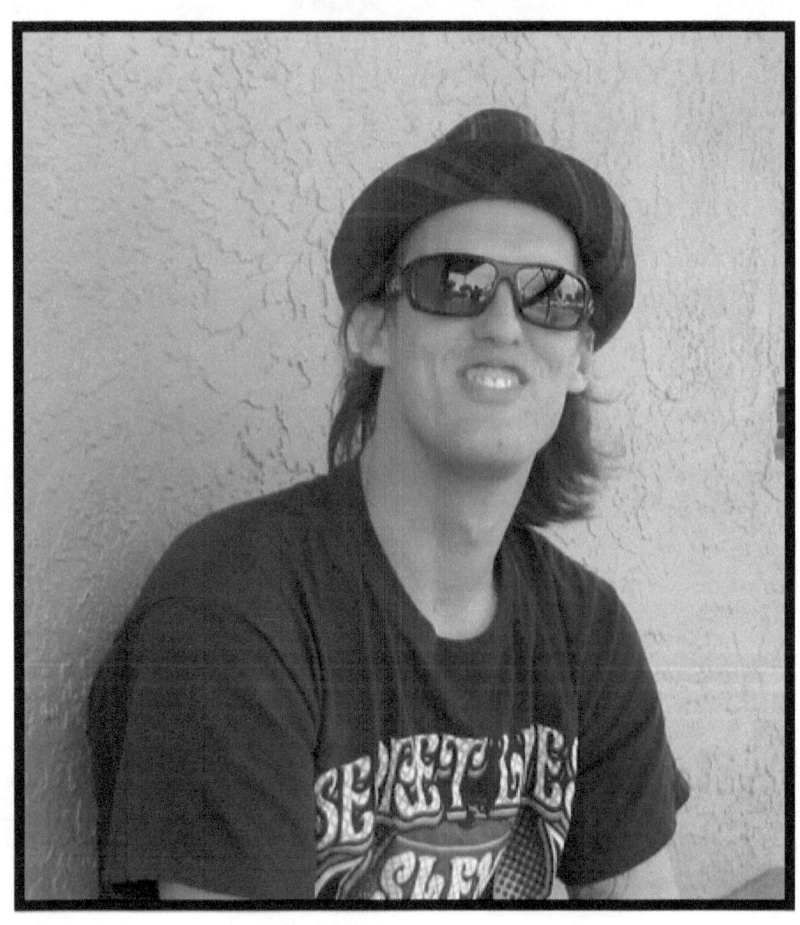

Mike, artist @ Tat2times Inc.

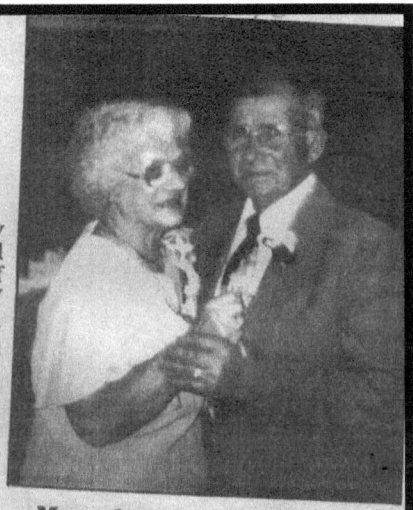

Mencarellis mark 50th anniversary

FRANKLIN — A 50th anniversary party was held recently for Mr. and Mrs. Carlo Mencarelli of Wachusetts Street at the VFW Post. The couple were married on Nov. 3, 1940. Mrs. Mencarelli is the former Caroline Bravo.

The party was hosted by Mr. and Mrs. Vincent Bravo of Medfield and several nieces and nephews. Relatives and friends attended from as far away as Florida.

Mr. and Mrs. Carlo Mencarelli

Mom and Dad @ their 50th wedding Anniversary
Rest in peace Mom and Dad
If only I knew then what I know now . . . .

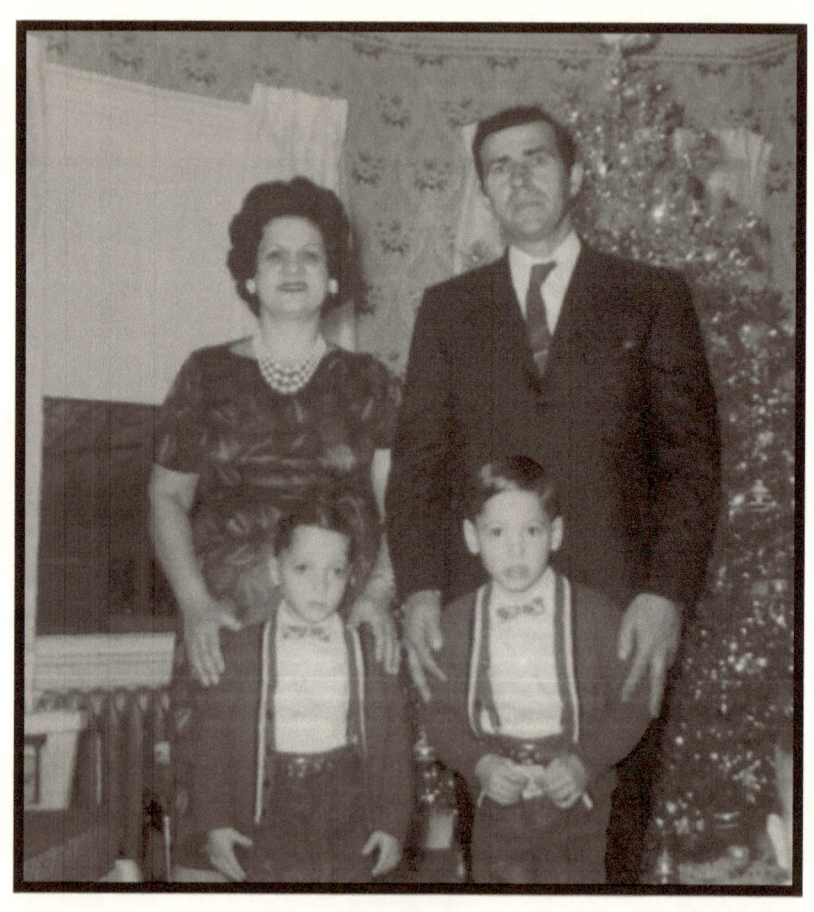

Mom, Dad, Walter, and me
Xmas 1968

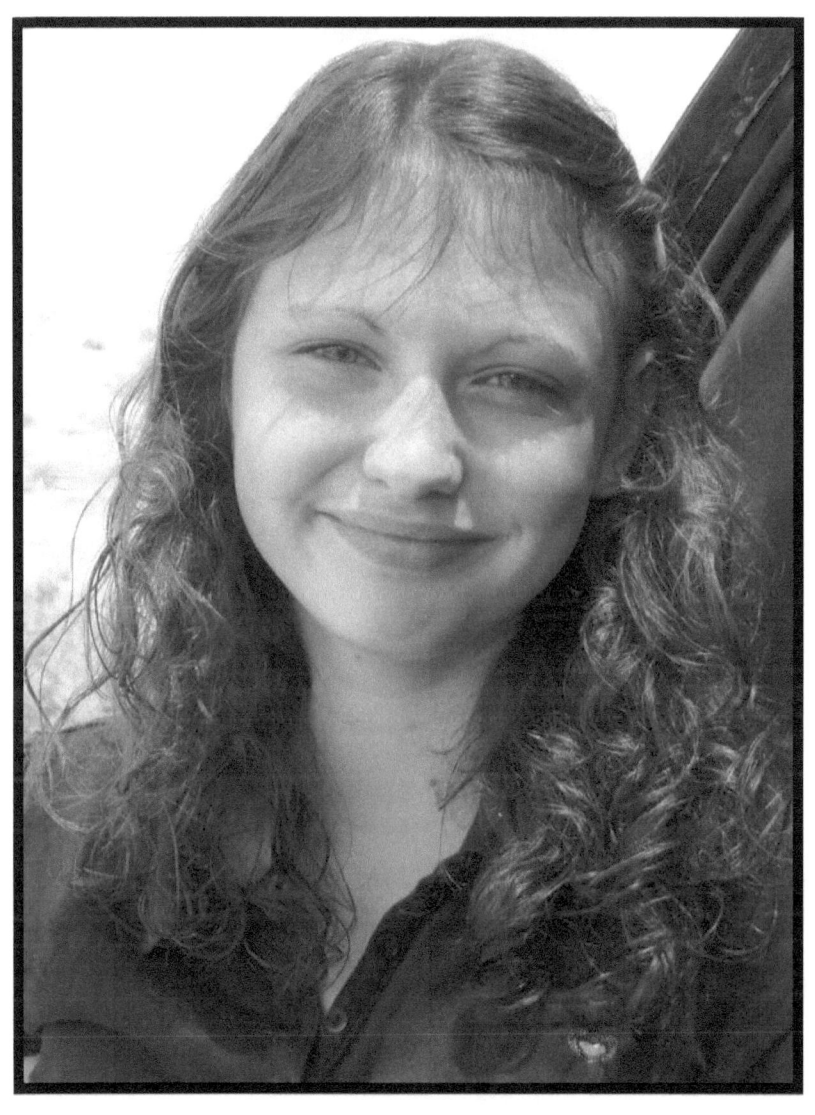

My Daughter Alecia, there isn't a day that goes by
that I don't think of her.

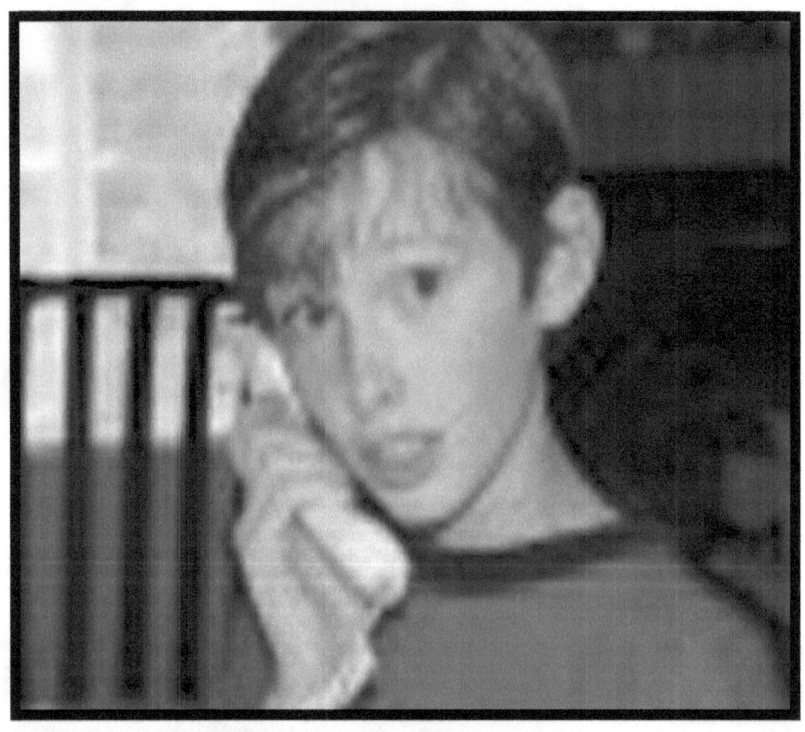

My son A.J. @ 15 years old

BEST OF
Palm Bay
2 0 0 8

TATTOOS & PIERCING

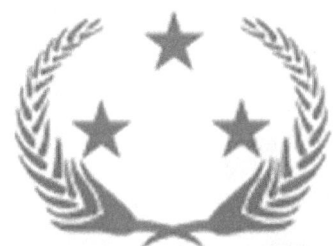

TAT2TIMES STUDIO 2
US LOCAL BUSINESS ASSOCIATION

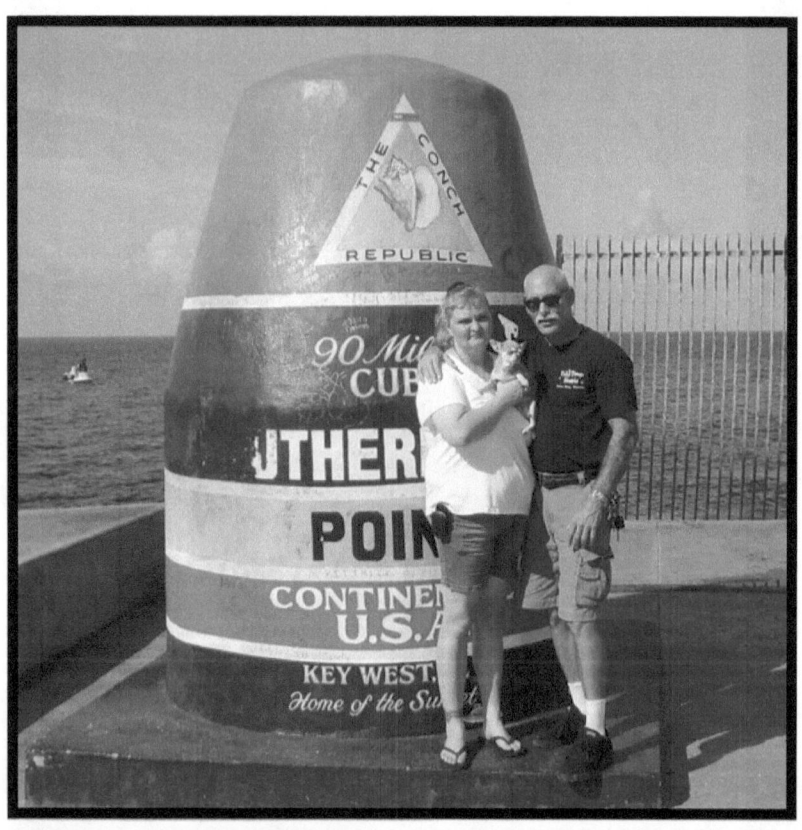

My wife, Patty and me @ the southernmost point in
Key West. Photo was taken a couple of months before
we made our proposal to the city for Key West Ink.

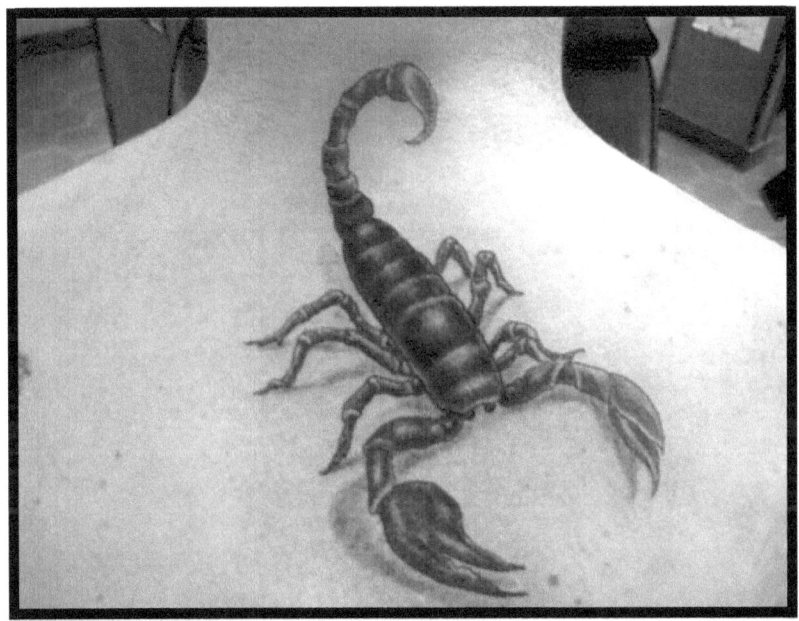

Collector unknown, another of many tattoo's done down @ KWI

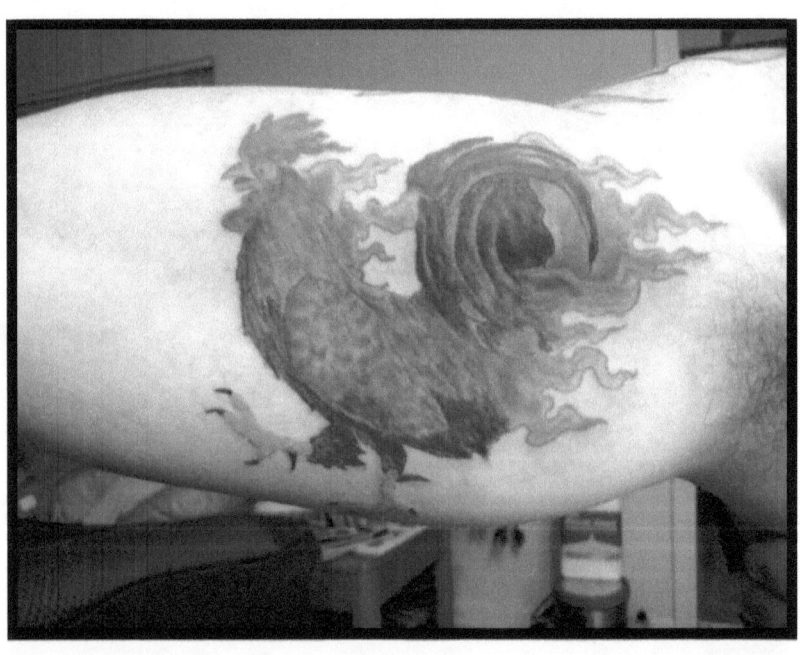

Sgt. H with tattoo drawn in memory of his brother.

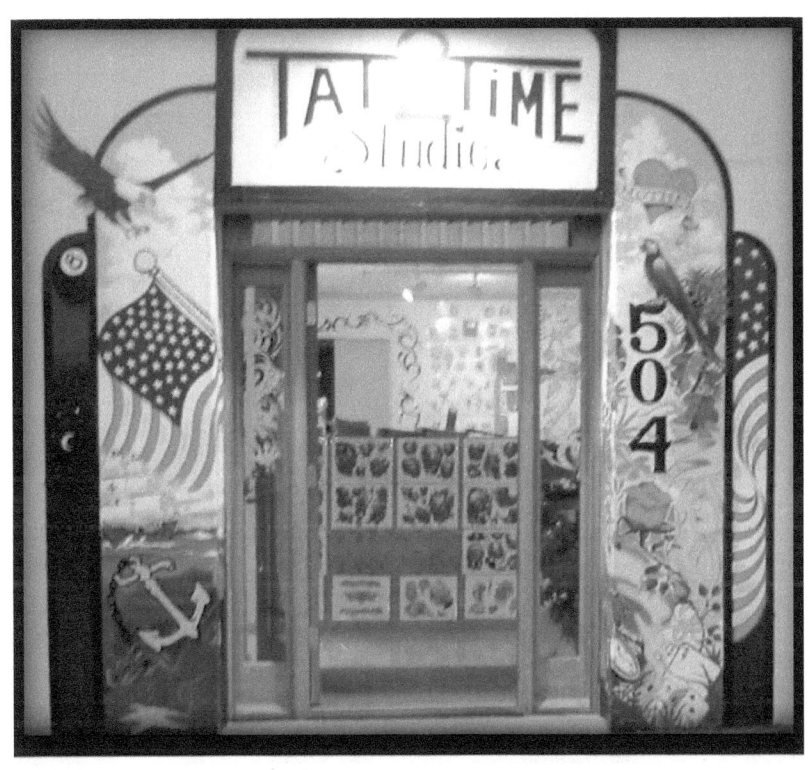

My studio front up in Olympia Wa.

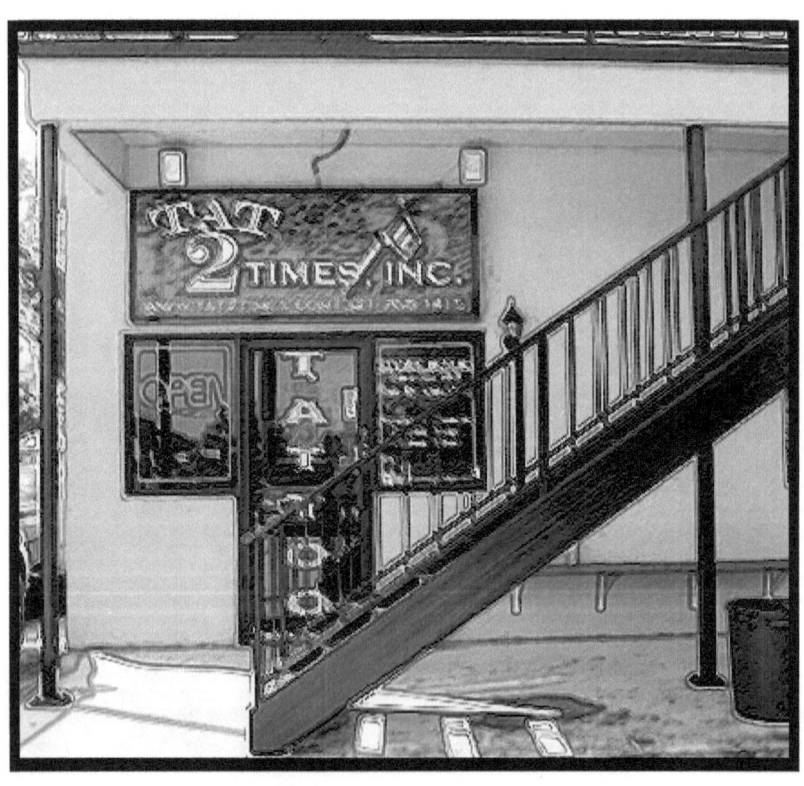

Tat2times Inc. Palm Bay, Fl.

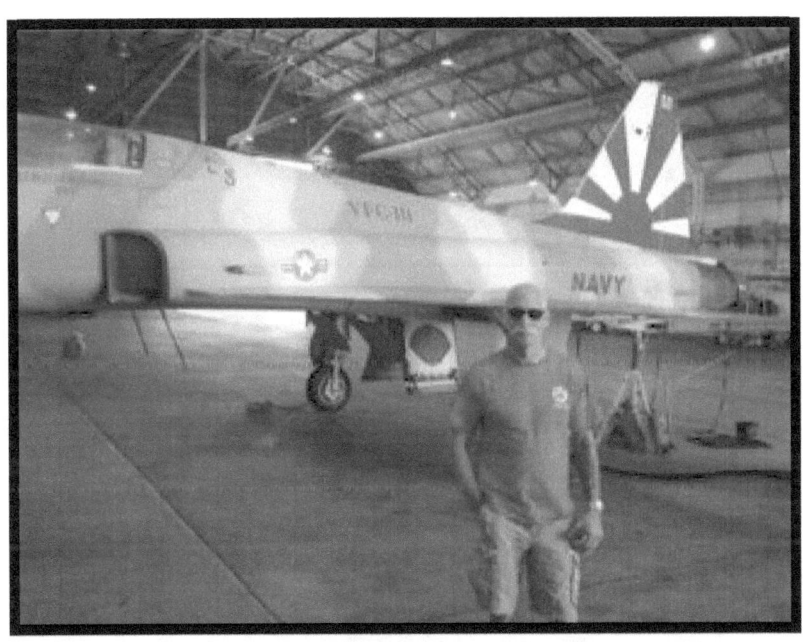

Boe in side hanger while on a
VIP tour @ Key West Naval Air Station

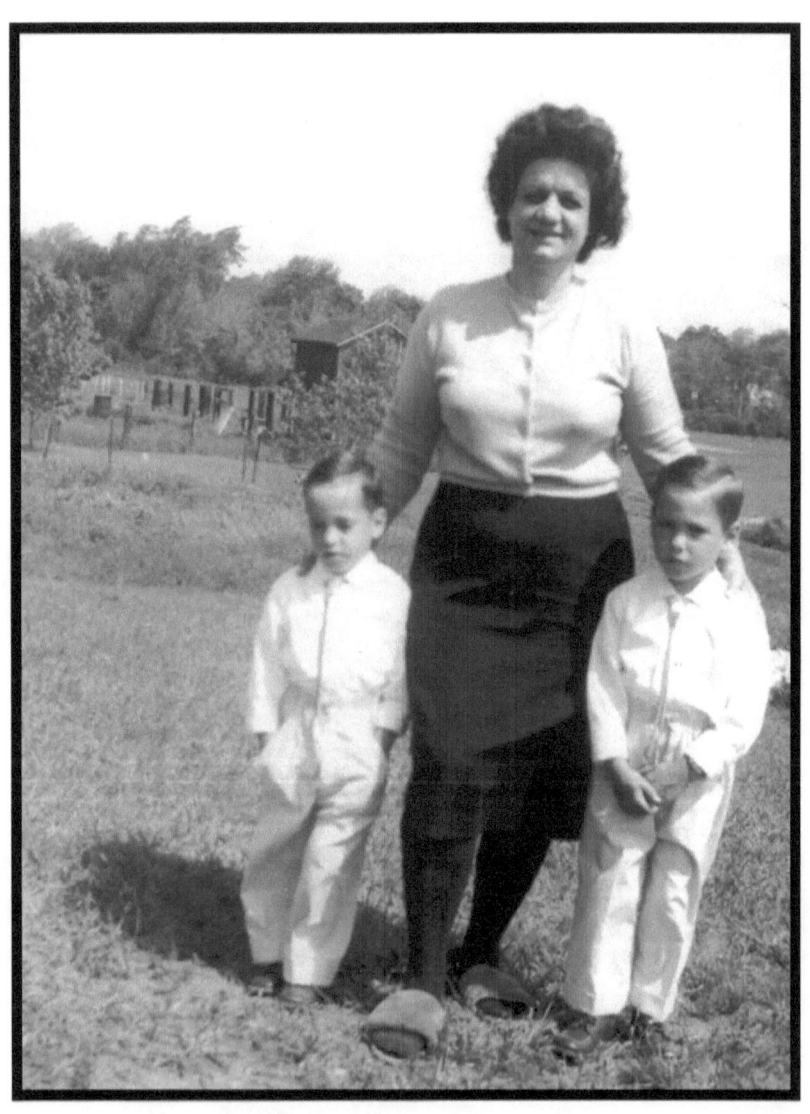

Walter and I with Mom Kay
June 4, 1962

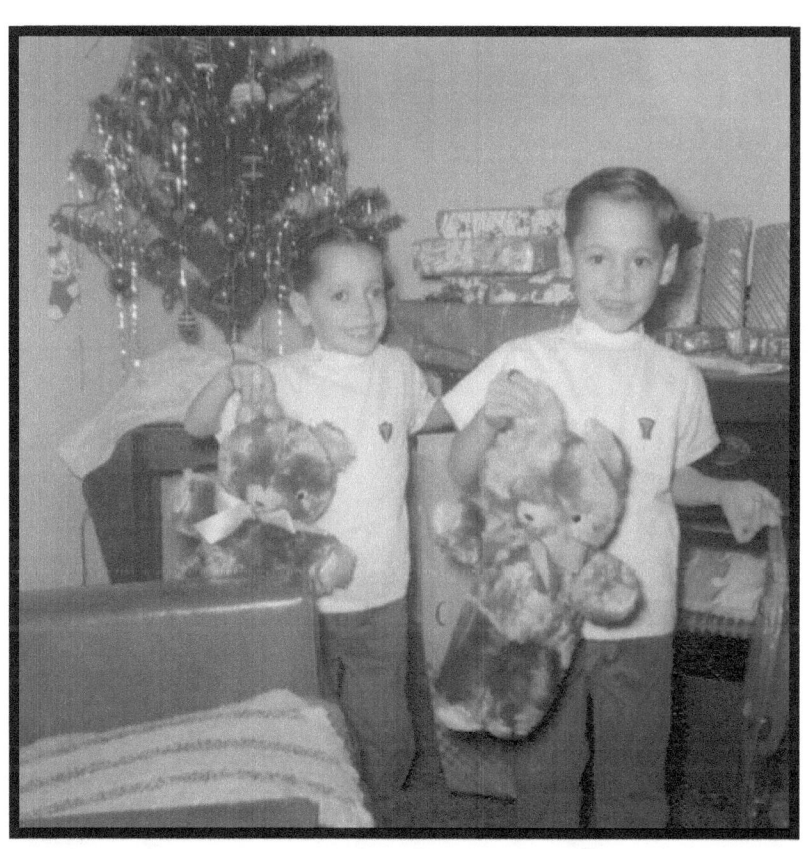

Walter and me, Xmas 1962

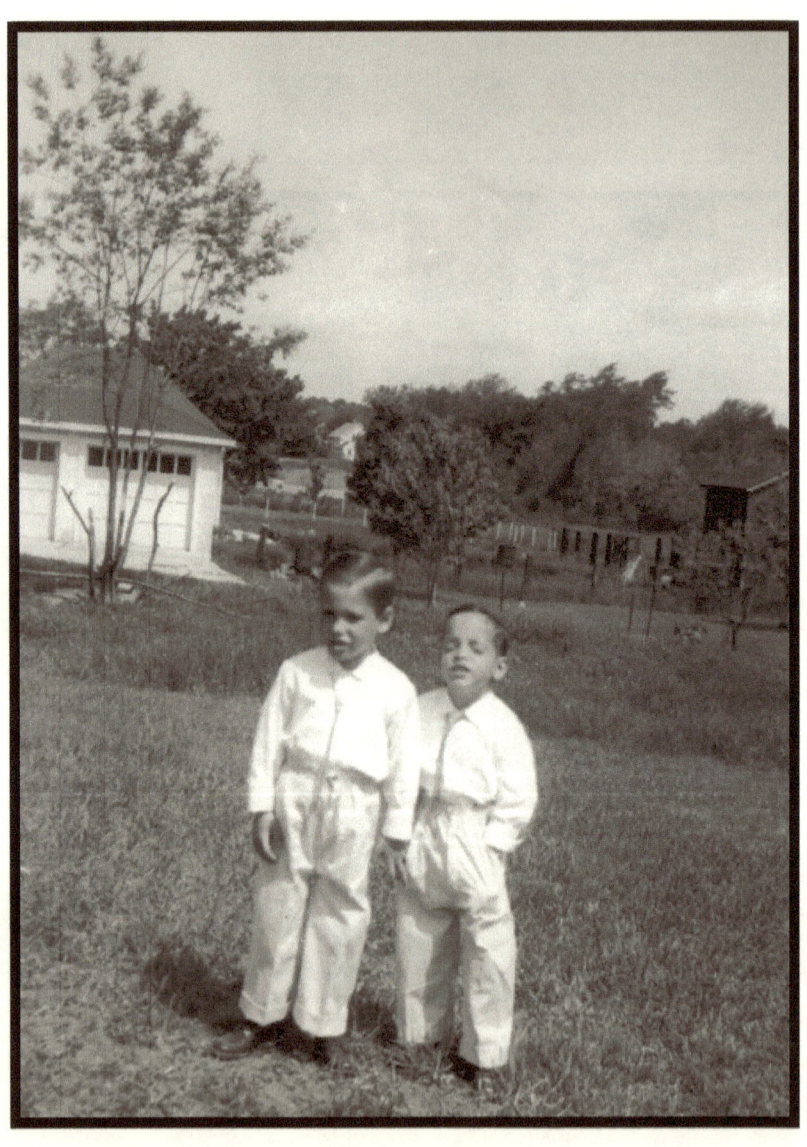

Me on the left and my brother Walter on the right.
June 4, 1962

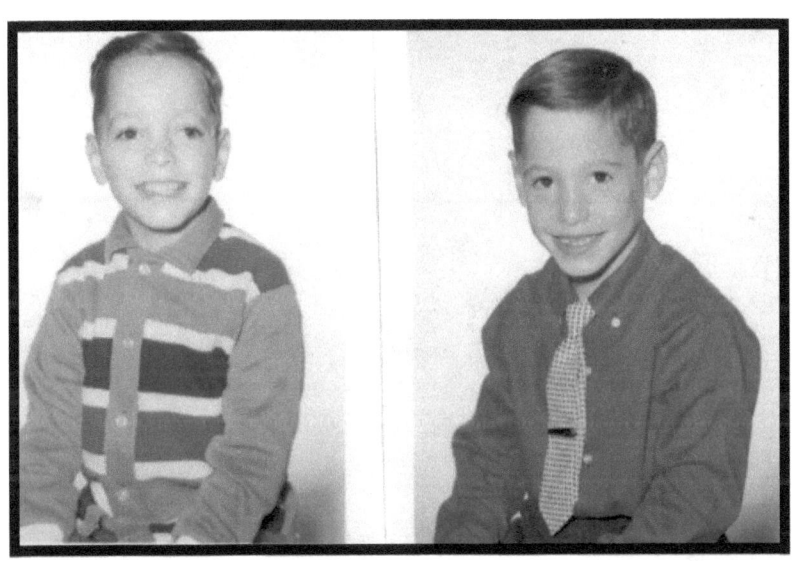

Walter and Me school picture

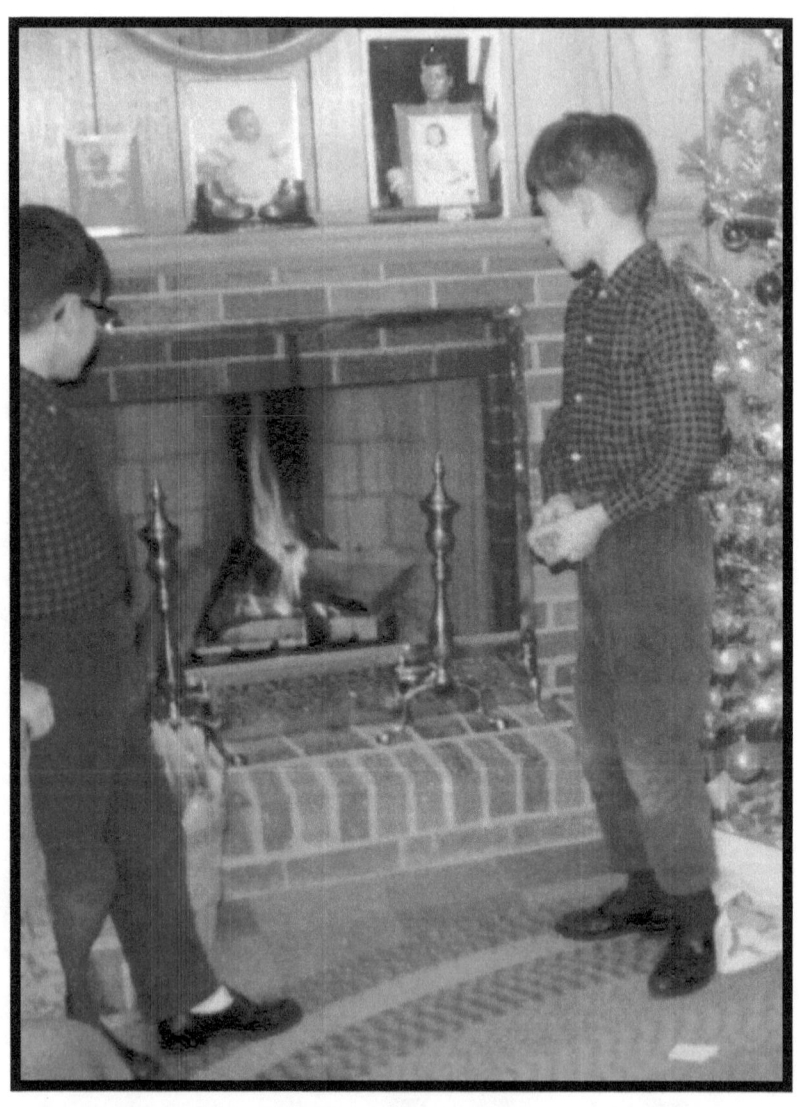

My brother Walter and me @ 9 years of age.
Waiting on Santa.

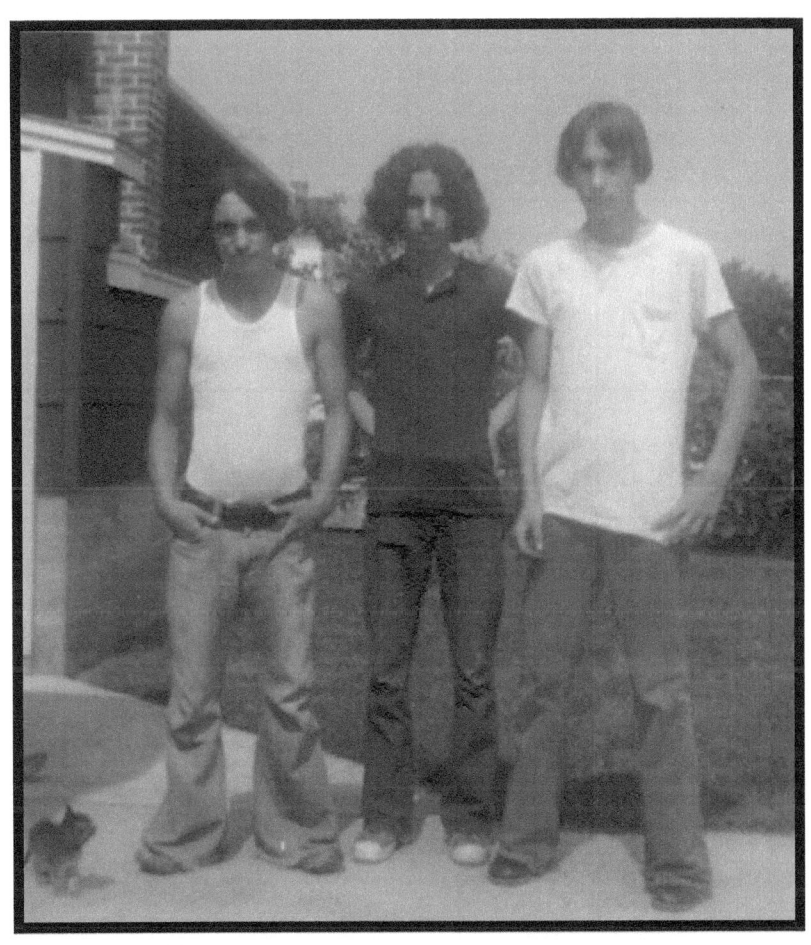

Walter, Donald Paladini and me. 1973

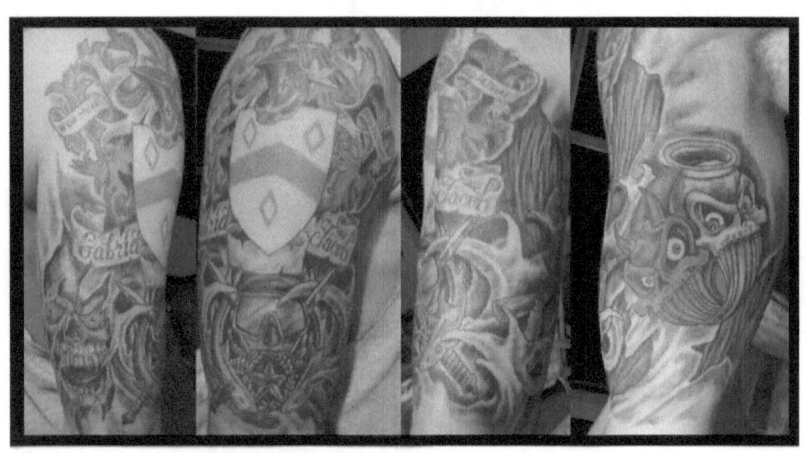

Picture of "Wild Man Jake's" right arm.
We knocked out this half sleeve in (3) sittings.

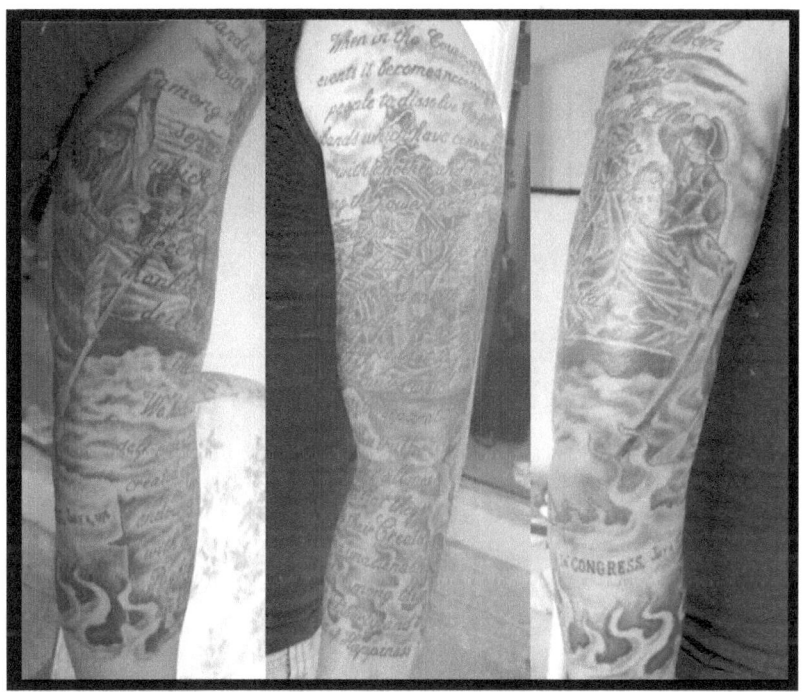

Collector Willy P . . . 1st three lines of the Declaration of Independence with an image of Washington crossing the Delaware. The thing that made this tattoo tough was, we did the writing part before the graphics. Thanks Willy P. for the challenge.

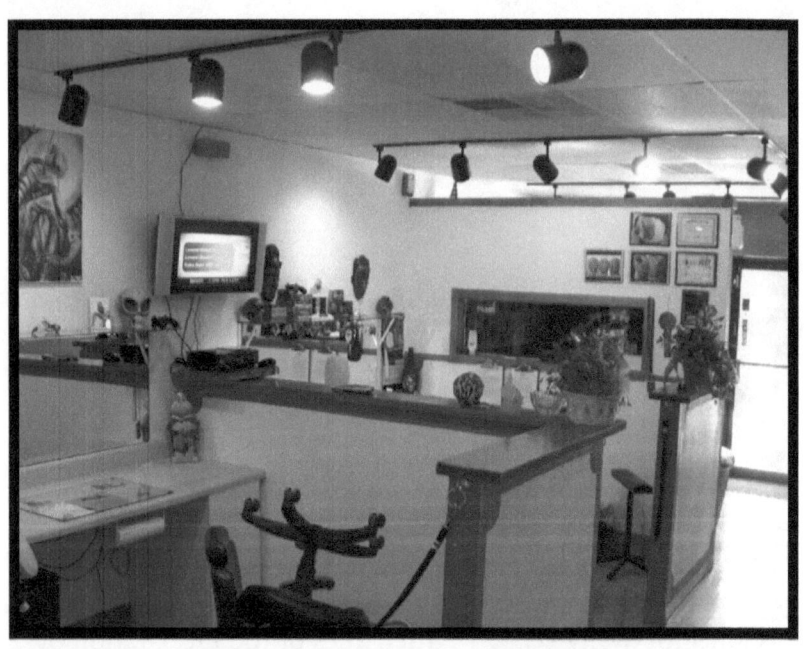

Workstation 1 and 2 @ Tat2times Inc.

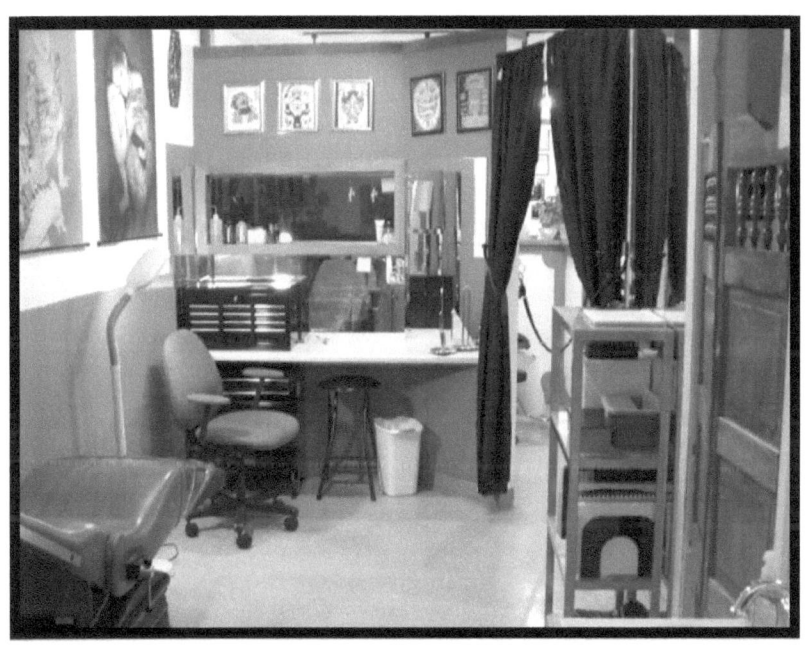

Workstation 3 @ Tat2times Inc.

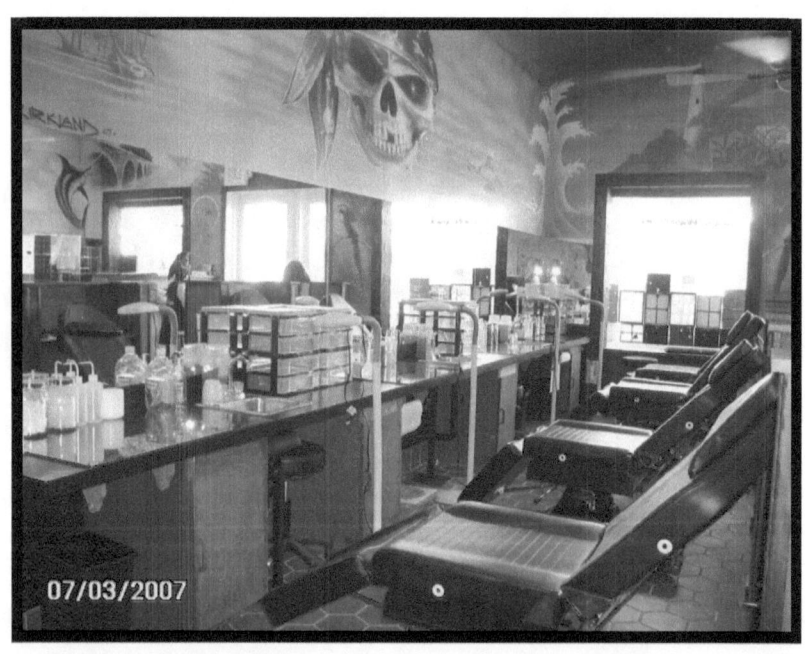
07/03/2007

Work stations 1 thru 4 @ Key West Ink

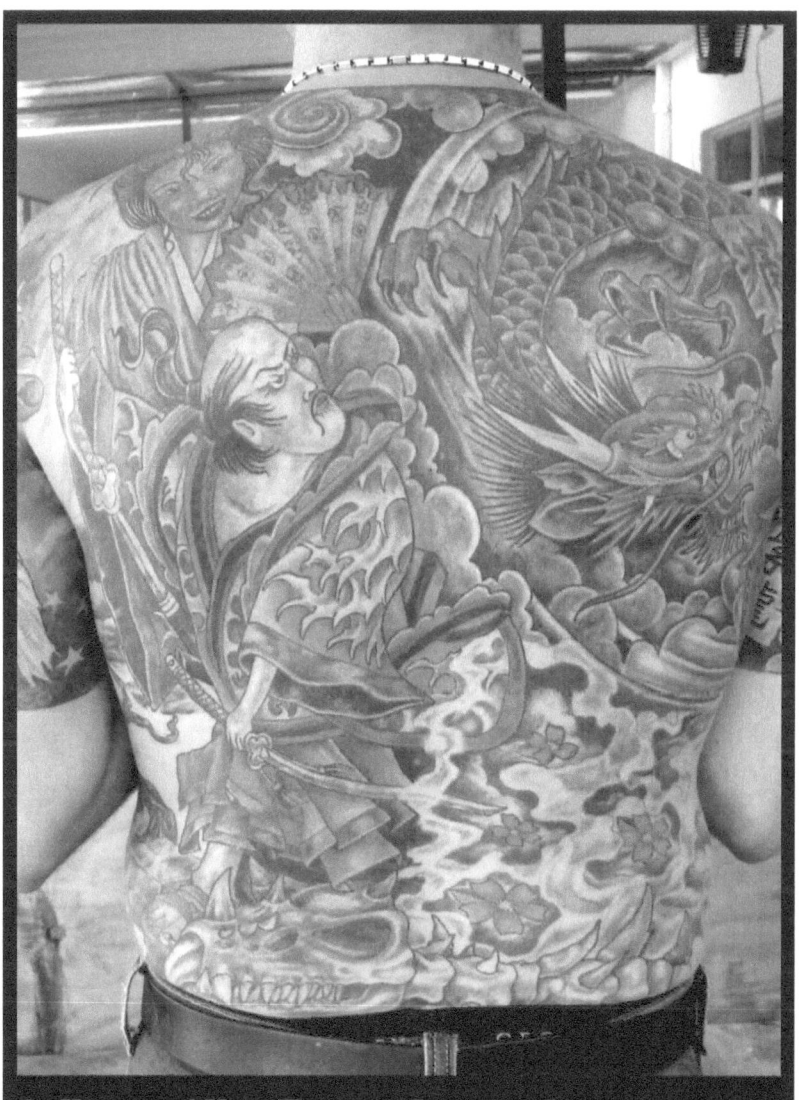

Collector Allen D. another work in progress

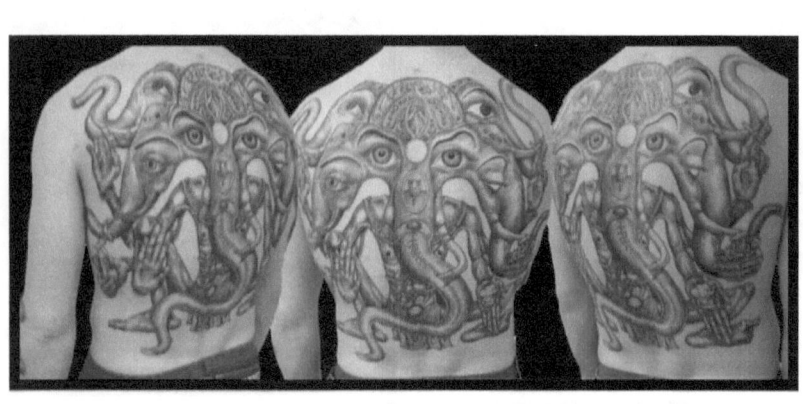

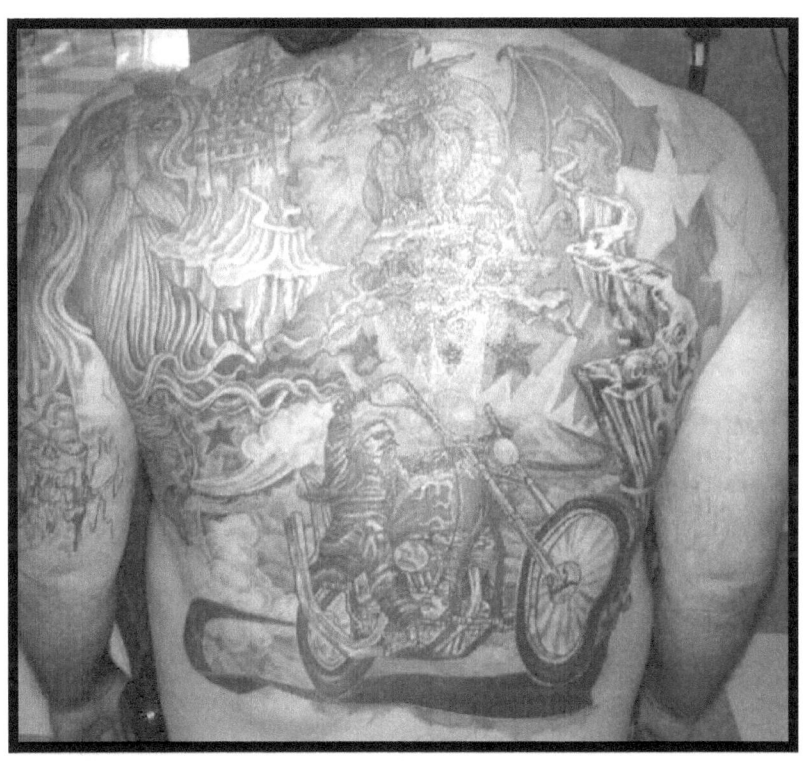

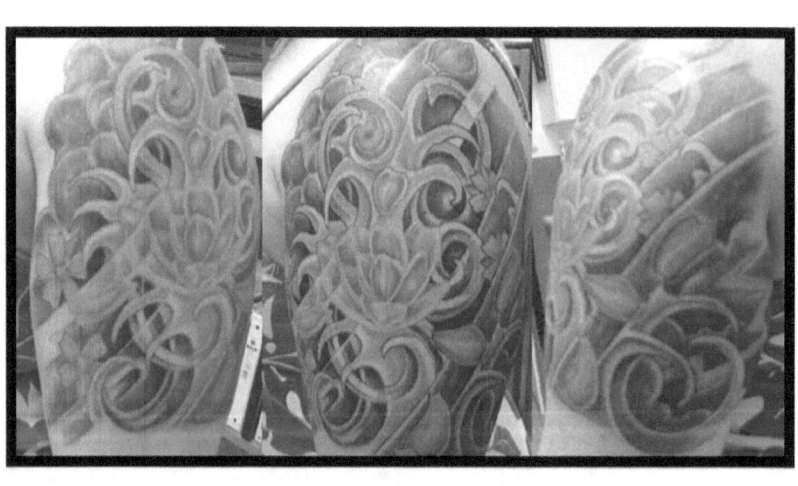

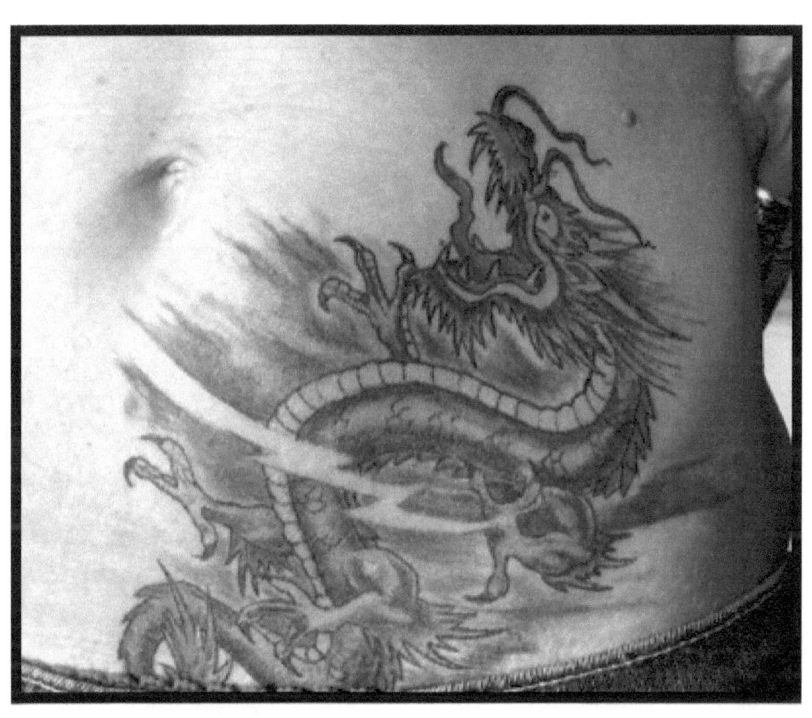

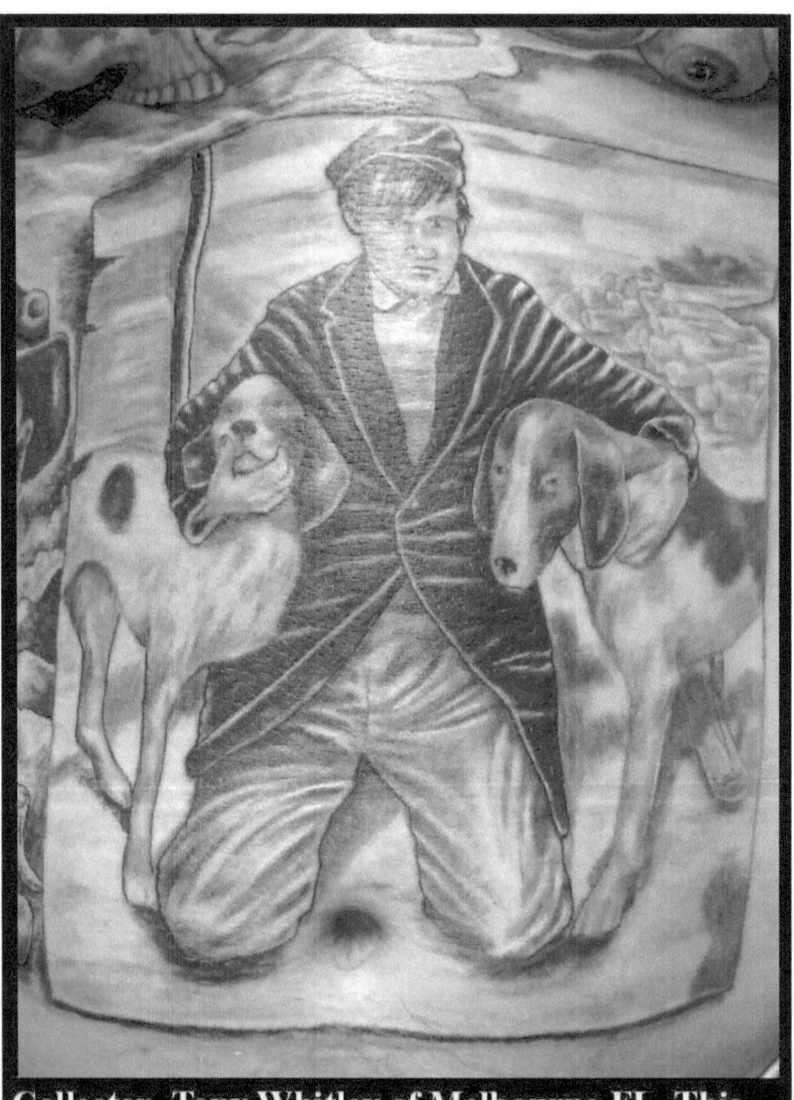

Collector- Tony Whitley of Melbourne FL. This picture is of his grandfather when he was 15 year old, the picture was taken in 1923

IV

When I got back from my trip to Olympia, I saw that John had called and I immediately got in touch with him. He wanted to stop by the next day, hash some things out about possibly opening a shop in Key West.

I was excited about the prospect, to say the least. I had had a partner in my business in Sacramento, and that had gone sour. However, I had a feeling that John was big money and very serious about his wanting to make good in Key West. Also, we had become pretty good pals and I thought I could trust him.

When he came in the next day, he plopped down in one of the customer's chairs and just looked at me with this shit eating grin on his face.

"Well, what did you find out?" I asked, just to be saying something. He was chewing on a toothpick and leaning back in the chair like he owned the place. With his newly tattooed skin, he could pass for a skin artist that is for sure.

"What do you say we become partners in this deal?" he asked. I shrugged, not sure what was expected of me.

"By partners, you mean what . . . 50/50?" I asked.

"51/49," he said. "My share being 51%"

I mulled this over. "How much is this gonna' cost me?"

"A buck," he said. "You can't beat that, can you?"

"You're not serious?" I grinned. "You're gonna' bring me in as a 49% share holder for a dollar?"

He laughed. "'Course, a lot will be expected of you, Boe. You'll have to help me set up the business, stock the shop with supplies and equipment, bring on staff. You know the good artists. I want only the best."

"Sounds like a game plan," I remarked, holding out my hand. We shook on the deal right then and there.

"Of course, I know you have your obligations here, and I wouldn't expect you to spend all of your time down South. But I will need a commitment from you that you will do everything you can to get this shop up and running. You are the expert, after all,"

"You have my word on it," I said that day.

There was a lot more research to be done regarding opening the Key West shop. We had decided on one thing so far, the name of the shop: KEY WEST INK. And we knew where we wanted the shop to be located: In the heart of Key West, on Duval Street. Now, there hasn't been a tattoo parlor anywhere near the city limits in Key West since 1966 and I knew it was going to be a hard sell to the local commissioners. It didn't matter that there were lap dancing parlors and seedy bars and T-shirt shops that blatantly displayed their wares with photos of every part of the human anatomy. Tattoos were just . . . taboo, had been for a long time. These old Key Westers (or Conchs, as they are called nowadays) were a hard sell, that I knew from the research I had done and the people I had talked to.

Both John and I wrote letters to the commissioners explaining our intention of opening the business. We wanted to get on the calendar for the next meeting. The mayor at the time didn't respond to our requests to talk with him until the producers of the acclaimed television show, Miami Ink called him about his thoughts on the business. And eventually, a couple of the commissioners did listen to us. Actually, one of the commissioners, a guy named Lopez, liked the idea of a tattoo establishment and sponsored our cause. That was pretty amazing, considering the conservative nature of the county governmental figures!

It had been three months since our initial discussion to make K.W.I. a reality. October was just a week away and we needed to set up some sort of shop prior to Fantasy Fest which was a popular event at the end of October. On October 6, 2006, John and I made our way up the long granite stairs attached to a red brick building that used to be City Hall. So it was that night that would prove to be the beginning of a long hard fight with the City of Key West. But we were optimistic. And we were determined.

As John and I stood in front of the podium, ready to state our case with our notes in front of us, we realized that the road was going to be very long indeed. The commissioners . . . most of them old time Key West residents . . . did not appear the least bit interested in what we were about to say. I was the first to speak. As I cleared my throat and began to talk, I felt that the commissioners were barely tolerating me, looking at their watches and around the room as if they couldn't wait to get out of there. Cocktail time in Key West . . . is it time to go yet?

John didn't fare much better. We had our facts and figures straight, we were articulate and courteous, but these folks just acted as if we were boring them to tears. Perhaps we were. Perhaps they were used to some fancy suited lawyer making a case for a client and we certainly did not look the part of affluent attorneys by any means. Both of us wore jeans, sported tattoos all over our skin and John wore his hair pulled back in his usual gray pony tail. Me, I wear my hair very short and have a rather large mustache and a mean expression when I am serious about something. And boy, was I serious about this! I am sure that they were looking at us as if we were a couple of idiots. Well, idiots make up a good part of Key West and hell, they do a damned good job of making money for the city at that!

After we had our say, we left the building and I told John that I thought we should hire an attorney. We needed one who was familiar with the first amendment because we believed that all forms of art are protected by the first amendment. So the next morning, first thing, we called Wayne Smith, a local attorney who specialized in this kind of law.

Smith is an articulate man, well groomed and well rehearsed in the law. His office was decorated with beautiful antiques and it was apparent to John and me that he was very successful. Mild mannered, slight in build, you wouldn't think he would be the type to take on the city. But he grew very excited as we explained what we wanted to do and why we wanted to do it.

"This is a new generation, Wayne," I told him. "There are a great many people with an eye for real art and they want to use their body as a canvas. This isn't the tattoos of the sixties and seventies; we're talking artistic value here!"

He agreed totally. He laid out some plans, told us up front what we would be up against, and outlined his fees. He had the kind of "fire in the belly" that we needed to get the job done and both John and I were sure we had picked the right man for the job.

As most everyone knows, October in Key West means one thing: Fantasy Fest. It is almost as popular as the famed Mardi Gras in New Orleans. What John and I wanted more than anything was to have a tattoo studio of some sort in place prior to and during Fantasy Fest. This would be the beginning of greatness for Key West Ink as we would have great exposure to the locals and the tourists alike. So we visited some properties on the street we were most interested in, Duval. This was *the street* as far as businesses and bars go, the main drag. A couple of property brokers, J. Myers and his assistant V. Dunbar knew of some places that would be perfect for us. The first building was interesting and would have been a good location, but we couldn't come to terms. The second building was in a great location at 717 Duval Street. This would eventually become the home of Key West Ink. But we still had a long, hard fight ahead of us in order to get it up and running.

Being visible during Fantasy Fest was important to John and me because we would be able to participate in the body painting, if not actual tattooing and we would be able to introduce our planned studio to the masses. What finally happened is that we were able to rent 717 Duval Street as our storefront for five days during the fest. It would cost us five grand, which is a lot of money for five days, but we thought it would be worth it. The upcoming week long party would mean a hell of a lot of work for me because I was in charge of putting together a couple of air brush stations, including all of the paints and supplies that go with it. Because we couldn't legally operate as a "tattoo" studio, we were relegated to offering body air brushing and henna painting, a form of non-permanent tattoo. So I purchased crates of body paint, airbrush paints, air brushes, tables and whatever I thought we would need to pull this off. The equipment and supplies put me back about three thousand dollars, but I figured that was nothing compared to the income we would make at the fest. I knew that eventually I would see a large part of the profits going into my pocket. Or so I thought.

Fantasy Fest is one big party after another. There are parades and individual parties at bars and restaurants. Let me tell you, I have never seen so many naked bodies in one place together and most of these people were drunk or on drugs. Every body type, every age were represented. It was crazy. People from all over the United States as well as from all over the world attended as it is known as a one of a kind event, crazy to the core. I am not an air brush artist per se, but I have been an artist my whole life and I have slung enough ink that it didn't take me long to get the hang of it. People left the shop happy with the work I had done and John couldn't be happier with the outcome.

"We did it!" he said excitedly. Of course, I was thinking to myself *we?* I'm not even sure he was anywhere around our booth the whole time! I was handing out flyers, helping my artist I'd hired with the body paint, pitching Key West Ink as if my life depended on it. As for John, well, he did sell me 49% of the upcoming business for a buck. Guess

I shouldn't complain. But already, there was this gnawing feeling in my gut . . .

After Fantasy Fest was over for the year, I was exhausted from lack of sleep, over worked, and broke. I think I had talked to thousands of people about our studio which we hoped to open within a short period of time. I got to the point where I think I was talking to my pillow when I did finally get to lay my head down.

I was broke because my "partner" decided he should keep the profits for all the air brushing I had done. And to top it off, I ended up paying a guy out of my own pocket that I had brought in to help, an artist from my studio in Palm Bay, Tat2times, Inc. Not only did I pay him $800.00 for his work, but I had to pay for his girlfriend's bus ticket to Key West because he was "home sick". Now, I am usually not a sucker for things like this, but I do tend to have a big heart and on more than one occasion, I have gotten the short end of the stick because of it. But still I felt I would eventually be able to make some money on this venture, if I just hung in there with John. In the meantime, I would have to count on my earnings from the Palm Bay parlor to tide me over and I just hoped that we could get the commissioners to come to their senses and see things our way. Our attorney seemed to think we had a strong case. I only hoped he was right. And I hoped I was wrong about my suspicions regarding John.

V

Six months passed and we were still getting the run around from the city. We decided to take it to the next level which meant we filed with the circuit court. Actually we had several court dates but on two occasions, we decided to put the brakes on it in hopes that the city would get on board and pass the new ordinance allowing tattooing inside the city limits. Because if we took it to court and the judge ruled in our favor, that would open the flood gates and allow any and everyone who wanted to open a tattoo studio to do so inside the city limits. We wanted the city to have some control and we presented it that way . . . none of us wanted a hundred tattoo studios popping up everywhere like the hundred or so T-shirt shops sprouting up on every corner.

We managed to get the zoning department to approve it with a little help from the inside. It is amazing the inner workings of the local government of small towns. If you know the right people and fill the right pockets, you can get most anything done. This is true not just of Key West, mind you. It is true of most smaller governments.

Now that I think of it, there was very little opposition from the people of Key West to our planned venture. For the most part, it was the commissioners who were responsible for dragging their feet. I guess they never thought we would have the staying power, they figured we would just give up and go away like a couple of pesky flies. Hah! Little did they know the perseverance they would encounter with John and me as well as our attorney. John had already purchased the property at 717 Duval Street along with a real estate partner. He wasn't going to take any chances of losing that deal. And I was in for the long haul, no matter that I felt John had screwed me out of income during Fantasy Fest. I was sure I would make it all back plus some. I was bound and determined to see this through, although my Palm Bay parlor was suffering and I was losing money because of it. I was spending a hell of a lot of time in the Keys, but I knew it was necessary in order to get this project done and get it done right.

Eventually I had to sell my studio in Washington State, just to get some pocket money to keep me afloat while I saw the Key West project through. It had become a burden on me anyway, and I had been thinking of getting rid of it for some time. The Palm Bay store ran itself, although without my supervision and without my artistic talents, the money wasn't coming in like it had been. But all I could envision was big bucks from Key West Ink. It was so exciting to be a part of something like this, making history and reading your name in the local and Miami newspapers. Almost every week there was an article in Key West's Citizen or the Keynoter. The Miami Herald had run a couple of great articles including photos of John and me which helped promote our shop.

Even the negative articles, written by a couple of the commissioners who were against the shop, helped our cause.

Sometime later, the city commissioners asked the city attorney to hold a work shop and bring back the findings at the next city meeting. The work shop was to go over our plans and ideas, how the studio would affect the town, and so on. We basically re-hashed the proposed ordinance that was actually put together by John and me. And believe it or not, all we did for the most part was pull up the city's ordinance on adult entertainment and substituted the words "tattoo establishments"! Sure, there were other stipulations regarding state and federal standards for tattoo studios, but more or less, our ordinance was almost word for word the same as that for the adult businesses. It was funny when the city attorney said what a great job John and I had done putting together the drafted ordinance! He even went as far as asking," Who did it for you?", thinking our attorney had probably had a hand in writing it. Little did he or the commissioners know it was their very own ordinance with a tweak here and there.

Two weeks after the work shop we were penned in on the calendar to go another round with the commissioners. We thought we had finally made some head way, that we had put together a workable ordinance that would make everyone happy. The city would be in control of the tattoo industry as far as standards go and they would oversee the process of new tattoo businesses coming into town, wanting to rent or buy space downtown. So we couldn't imagine how they would object this time around. But once again they managed to throw another wrench into the system. The commissioners came up with a lame excuse that they thought a number of the commissioners should have attended the work shop and now they wanted to rehash the whole ordinance approval.

We had about eight months wrapped up in this fight by the time another meeting was scheduled. This time, Paradise Tattoo (which had a studio on Stock Island, a couple of miles away over Cow Key bridge) wanted to approach the commissioners about getting a studio opened on Duval at the same time we opened ours. The owners of that studio started hassling us, saying they thought the work stations in our shop were too close together. They claimed we did not have a barrier wall separating the work stations, which they said was necessary for health and privacy. Basically, they were just bitching because they felt we were about to win our bid to open K.W.I. and they wanted their shop to be able to open in the city, also. They wanted to make us as miserable as possible in the process.

Paradise Tattoo owners actually tried to have it written in the statutes that tattoo work stations would be mandated to have a half wall, dividers or some other type of barrier between the stations. If the city mandated this, Paradise knew that K.W.I. would have to go back in to do major construction of the interior of our building. This would involve permits and cause more delays. They were only hurting themselves in the long run because they were trying to open up on Duval Street also. Any building they chose would have to meet the same criteria. However, there were so many "nonsense" comments from the Paradise Tattoo people that even the commissioners were getting sick of them. They saw what was going on. Their greed was leaving a bad taste in the mouths of everyone involved.

Something did work out in our favor however, in the months waiting on the city. While we were biding our time, we began renovations on 717 Duval Street. After all, John owned the place now and there was nothing to keep us from beginning the work which was necessary to get our business up and going when things finally did get settled. John, his son J.B. and I all went to work on the building, not waiting for permits in order to start construction. We blacked out the windows on the building so no one could see what was going on inside and started tearing down and renovating. John figured because he had a General Contractor's license that he wouldn't need to go through all the red tape involving permits and such. He eventually did file for permits, but not until we were almost done. It is amazing how he pulled that one off.

I remember being up about fifteen feet in the air on a scaffold, re-wiring all the lighting while John is down on the ground, yelling instructions to me. He was telling me which wires to connect and disconnect. Well, sure enough he did not know what the hell he was talking about and the next thing I remember was seeing this bright white light and my entire arm went numb. I came very close to electrocuting myself that day because of John's need to cut corners by not hiring a qualified electrician. Of course, it didn't matter that I had told him I wasn't up on electrical work. He just smiled and told me I could do it, why hire a professional when there was the "three" of us to do the work?

It took months to remodel the interior of K.W.I. The whole time, I slept on an air mattress up in the loft. With some changes to the interior wall, we placed a 3 X 5 window in it so the loft would be made into a working station/office. The view from up there was great. I lived up there for about five of the eight months it took to get the interior done. I didn't mind the saw dust as I had roughed it plenty while I was in the military in the infantry. Besides, we had been receiving some threatening e-mails in the recent weeks and I thought it was best that someone keep an eye on the place at night.

I got involved in hiring some artists to do the mural work inside the studio on the walls and on the ceiling. A lot of them offered to do this gratis, as they just wanted to show off their art work to the public and be a little part of the history that was K.W.I. Most of the time I felt as if I were babysitting, trying to get these guys to show up on time if they showed up at all. Key West is a very laid back town and the people there, especially the artistic types, are very laid back also. They did things on their time or what I started calling "Key West Time".

I had this one artist who e-mailed me, called me every other day, begging me to allow him to do a mural on the walls of the shop. All he could talk about was how great he was with an air brush. He ended up being a good artist but the guy had so much baggage that half way through the thirty five days it took to finish the mural, I was ready to call it quits. For one thing, he couldn't work unless he had at least one six pack in him. I think if he had put as much effort into spraying paint as he had chasing down his next drink, we could have shaved two weeks off that 35 day nightmare. Actually, a couple of weeks into his paint job, he ended up sleeping on the dirt covered floor because it was more comfortable than sleeping in his car. He didn't have a place to call home and I felt a little sorry for him, but he drank away any money he made. So it was his own damned fault. It was hard for me to understand how a thirty-nine year old guy with so much talent could be living out of his car. We all make choices, that is for sure, and his was to spend his adult life in the bottom of a bottle. He had an extreme case of the "poor me" syndrome. The way I look at this is, I can't help you if you can't help yourself and the maximum effective range for an excuse is Zero meters and Santa Claus really doesn't exist and the gravy train went on strike so it is time get off the dummy ride and take some responsibility.

I think the two people who stand out the most in opposing what we were trying to accomplish were the owners of Paradise Tattoo. I can remember the very first commissioners meeting when we made our initial proposal to the city where the owners of Paradise Tattoo were in the audience, ready to oppose our idea of opening the shop. "G" and "D", as I will refer to them here, were quick to stand at the podium bad mouthing the idea of allowing tattooing within the city limits of Key West when ten years ago, they had made an attempt to do the very same thing. John and I actually met with them prior to making our proposal because we thought it would be best to have them onboard with our request. But they weren't onboard . . . they were upset because their shop, located a couple of miles North on Stock Island, would lose a lot of business if K.W.I. ever came to be a reality. And they were not at all sure they would be given the privilege of opening their own studio in Key West proper.

Going against another artist in this business is pretty much unheard of, at least these days. We usually support one another and learn from each other. But not in this case . . . they wanted to play dirty and we would play dirty right back if we needed to.

The moral part of it still does not make sense to me. But then there is the other factor, the one thing that will change a person quicker than anything else in this life and that is the almighty dollar. Greed will come back around to bite you in the ass if you aren't careful. Paradise Tattoo would experience this sometime in the future.

After a conversation with a well known Key West banker who clued me in that Paradise Tattoo had shown credit card sales in the neighborhood of $600,000.00 the previous year, excluding cash sales, it appeared that they were afraid of losing a lot of money if Key West Ink became a reality. People who came to Key West would no longer need to travel to Stock Island for their tattooing needs. A lot of tourists didn't even know about the shop on Stock Island in the first place, but they still did a hell of a business. So Key West Ink posed a major threat to Paradise's profits and they would do anything short of breaking the law to see that our shop never opened. D., G.'s partner and wife at Paradise, even went as far as telling the commissioners at one of the first meetings that one of our artists had threatened them via an e-mail correspondence. It was an Oscar winning performance, the tears and the quivering, you had to be there to appreciate the drama. Now get this: G. had moved to Key West some thirteen years prior to all of this taking place. He worked on a fishing boat and one day, a new deck hand came to work with a fresh tattoo. G. asked where he had gotten it and worker told him he had

had it done at Goldie's Tattoo, one of the first tattoo shops to open on Stock Island. The deck hand told G. what he paid to have the tattoo done and G. made up his mind that very minute to get into the tattoo business himself. So he tossed his fishing poles and picked up a tattoo machine. No apprenticeship, no art background. Just an instant self-proclaimed "Rock Star" status as a great tattooist. Only in America, I say. Money signs flashed before his eyes and there we go again . . . the big green Greed sign.

Things are different today as opposed to thirty years ago. Tattooing has become a near fashion statement and because of this trend, there are a lot of people in the industry that really have no business being there. It is my belief that you should at least have the ability to draw in order to obtain a tattoo license. But that is not the case anymore. You will find many people owning a shop or working in one with no art background at all. And it is these people who still give tattooing a bad name. You see it all the time. There is a huge difference between a well thought out work of art done as a tattoo and something that has just been slapped on without a solid concept of the work to be done.

Then there is the other side of the coin: Because of the popularity of tattooing, individuals with degrees in fine art who have chosen to step into the skin art arena bring with them the skills of that education, and by doing so have increased the quality of skin art today. There are some fine tattoos out there. Many of them are very individualistic and well inked, and can be rather expensive to boot. But these are works of art done by professionals, not by fly-by-night tattooists who consider them selves to be artists of some sort or another.

It is a great time to be in this business, I have to say. Images are being brought to life on skin that were never dreamed of thirty years ago. It is truly amazing and I am proud to be a part of it. Taking on the city of Key West energized and ignited my passion for my art. We would be making history if we could just get the city to approve our shop. Forty some years is a long time for minds to be closed to something that is so prevalent and popular today. And certainly, our professionalism would stand out among the crowd.

But again, we had opponents who were adamant about their negative take on our project and if they had any real pull, Key West Ink might not come to fruition. We would be a tattoo studio without any tattooing. That didn't set right with John or me. And we were determined to overcome the obstacles, come hell or high water.

VI

There came a time when the media went a little crazy with the idea of our opening up the first tattoo studio to hit Key West property in over forty years. John and I both gave interview after interview to newspapers and television stations alike. I think the story made seventy newspapers world wide. It was crazy. Everyone I talked to while promoting Key West Ink seemed incredulous that we were having to go through so much turmoil with the city to get the license to open. "My, God! Are you kidding? Key West has to be the most liberal city in the country!"

Key West Newspaper Citizen comments

10/29/06
   "I just walked by the 900 block of Duval Street with my family. They've got girl's panties with explicit statements right in the window, and they're worried about tattoo shops"

There were literally thousands of people I spoke with from July 2006 until the day we finally opened on August 22, 2007. These were people from all walks of life. From the rich and famous to the humble and poor. People from all over the world . . . Japan, China, England, Scotland, South Africa . . . and the list goes on. Come to think of it, I did about 90% of the promotion work at 717 Duval because I was the guy who really knew the tattoo business. It was my work that was being displayed throughout the studio or the work of the artists who worked for me. And those were my awards adorning the walls.

I think the most memorable award was one that I won at the 2004 Seattle tattoo show. It was about that time that the industry lost a legend in the business. His name was David Mann. For those of you who don't know who Mr. Mann was, he was responsible for all of the centerfold art in the Easy Rider Magazine for a long, long time. He was an incredible artist. I've done a number of his pieces on skin including a full back tattoo I did on a friend of mine named Scott. It was a piece depicting David Mann himself riding on a floating highway that went to nowhere. I was actually at my Palm Bay location when I got the call from Scott. He was ecstatic, screaming happily into my ear.

'We did it, Boe!" he yelled. "We took first place in the "Best Color, Male" category!"

That was one big upper, let me tell you, a real reason to celebrate. The Seattle show is one of the classiest around and I couldn't help but grin from ear to ear as I heard Scott exclaiming.

We had started the artwork on Scott about seven months before the show with the idea that he would attend in order to gain recognition for the art. Well, sure enough, he had pulled it off and I have to admit, I was a little surprised because there were a couple of hundred artists taking part in the show. I mean some really great artists from shops like "The Electric Rose", "Slave to the Needle", "Tat2-U" and "Black Pearl", just to mention a few. Thousands of people attended the Seattle show every year. There would always be some outrageous ink being shown there but of course, Seattle is known for its art scene.

I had once managed a studio in Seattle . . . I love that city, it is full of life and buzzing with creativity. The shop I managed was called "Art Attack". The owner got caught up in some sort of bad scene and had to take a "vacation", so to speak. So I ran the place for almost a year. I did not know at the time that the city of Everett was trying to shut down the studio. Prior to my taking over the management, it did appear that the shop had some things going on that had nothing to do with tattooing. The owner's girlfriend was in charge of overseeing the operations, doing the meet and greet thing, calling the numbers on most of the work being done. All I had to do really was sling ink. Yeah, I had to put together the art being done but other than that, she did everything else. Things like setting up and cleaning up weren't part of my job description. I would pick up the tattoo machine at about two in the afternoon and I didn't put it down until three a.m.!

The Art Attack closed down because supposedly the owner's girlfriend disappeared with all of the money made while he was gone, other than my salary. The city closed it down because the property the building sat on was sold to some congressman and he wanted to turn it into his office.

What a lot of people didn't know was that the tattoo studio sat next door to "The White Elephant", a popular biker bar and the headquarters of "The Banditos", a hard core bikers club. They wouldn't take shit from anyone. The Banditos and Hell's Angels have been feuding for years and there have been countless murders of members from both clubs. Knowing all of this did not make me feel extremely safe working at The Art Attack and it didn't bother me that it closed down.

Back to Key West: The second workshop was held and according to all parties concerned, the paperwork was finally in order and we found the tattooing issue on the calendar for the next commissioners meeting. It would be put to a vote. From our understanding, everything was supposed to fall into place for a change. Even some of the old blood who sat on the board of commissioners were seemingly okay with our ordinance. Actually, they held a special meeting just for this vote because the city had run out of time with this issue. We had a court date that was coming up fast and furious, and the city was deeply concerned that the judge would rule in our favor and grant our First Amendment right, freedom of expression. Sure enough the city voted and it passed. That was on August 21st, 2007. Part of the settlement with the city was the fact that K.W.I., along with Paradise Tattoo, would be allow to open and operate on Duval Street downtown. Because we would not have to go to court, no other tattoo studios could open in mainstream Key West, but would have to open on back streets only. Key West Ink came out of this meeting smelling like a rose because we were the so-called "underdog" here, the ones who took it to the city and after a bit of a battle, finally won. Because John owned the building on 717 Duval and did not just lease it, we were immediately grandfathered in. And Paradise Tattoo, although they could open on Duval as only the second shop allowed on that street, planned to lease a location. So if anything happened, and someone bought out their location, they would have to move. And that would mean moving to a new location . . . not on Duval.

I couldn't wait for the doors to open the next day. We had so many people waiting in anticipation for this historical event, it was unbelievable. One of the first people to sit in my chair was "Inga", (a.k.a. Roger Hultman) a local female impersonator who has been working in Key West for about eleven years. Some people know her as "The Sweedish Bomb Shell". She had been putting together ideas for a complete sleeve tattoo for months. She would convey those ideas to me and I in turn would transform those ideas into images.

I had completed all the prep work and was ready to begin moments after the doors would open. The turnout for the grand opening was phenomenal. K.W.I. was surely the center of attention. The news media was swarming the place. The Associated Press got a hold of the story and the rest just seemed to come out of the woodwork. In fact, one of the photographers for a local newspaper in Key West, The Citizen, earned a prestigious award for photograph of the year for his photo of Inga being tattooed by me that very first day.

By the end of that first, fabulous day, I for one was a tired dog. I had slung ink for twelve hours straight. Between that and all of the interviews, I was ready for some much needed rest. The next day was a repeat of the first: slinging a lot of ink, talking to the press, having pictures taken. It was truly a tattoo artist's dream come true. Being able to work a lot of hours in a city that is like none other in the United States was reward in itself. Watching people do the "Duval Crawl" (most with a drink in hand!) was a blast and checking out the latest passengers off the Key West layover cruise was always good for a laugh. This was heaven, as far as I was concerned.

After slinging ink on "Inga" for about six hours, the next guy in line for my chair was a guy I have gotten to known quite well. His name is Alan Dockery and some folks know him as Chief Dockery, Alan was a faithful follower of K.W.I. and what we were trying to do there. He had stopped by countless times to check on our progress with the city officials. I believe it was the second time that he came by that he showed me some art work he had done on his upper arm and shoulder area. By the look of the work, I thought surely I had known the guy responsible for that mess invading his skin. I believe his name was "Scratch Pad Willy" . . . a name relegated to the many wannabe tattoo artists in the industry. What was supposed to be a tattoo looked as if someone had taken an engraving tool to his arm. I felt bad for Allan because of the mess he had to walk around with showing on his skin. If I ever had had work done like that on me, I would take a shower with my shirt on just so I wouldn't have to look at it!

We made some pretty good progress that first day, fixing up the mess "Scratch" Pad had made. That first sitting was just the start of what would become not only a good friendship between Alan and me, but would also be one of countless sittings I'd spend with him.

The days and weeks that followed were pretty much like the first day, except that the press had backed off a little, which was a blessing in itself because with so many reporters and photographers hanging around, it was hard to get any work done. I was usually the first one in the shop, getting to work an hour before opening and being the last to leave. It wasn't uncommon for me to work sixteen hour days, seven days a week. I would go back to my home in Palm Bay about every two weeks, checking in on my other shop and making an appearance at my home because Patty saw very little of me during that time. Trying to keep my marriage on track was beginning to be difficult to say the least with me being gone so much. She wasn't too happy about it and I can't say that I blame her.

Well, Key West Ink was open about a month and I was working my ass off, putting in twelve to fourteen hour days but seeing very little money for my efforts. I was starting to become a little concerned because John hadn't given me my 49% shares he had promised. I should have received a certificate now stating that I owned a good portion of the business. But every time I would bring up the subject, John would come up with one excuse or another. This didn't sit well with me, that's for sure. John was more or less ignoring the fact that I was his partner.

One afternoon I had had enough of it and I confronted John about my shares. He said that the attorney would not do any more work for us because K.W.I. owed him $58,000.00! He told me the paper work had been started but would not be finalized until much of the debt was paid. He tried to tell me that the attorney would not accept payments and I thought that was odd. What attorney would not take payments on a bill that was nearly $60,000.00? At this time, I offered to give Mr. Smith $5,000.00 in hopes of getting him to finalize the paper work. Again, John gave me the runaround. It was about this time that I began to wonder if I wasn't being played for a fool and it was this thought of possibly being taken advantage of that enraged me. After all, I had spent a year of my life on the K.W.I. venture. I attended all the commissioners meetings, contributed thousands of hours of my time and knowledge not to mention about thirty grand of my own money in order to make our shop viable. Even after everything was in place . . . equipment, artists, etc . . . I gave John countless hours of my time when he decided to buy a duplex on Angela Street. I worked without pay seven days a week, ten and twelve hours a day helping to remodel a very old, rundown Victorian house which sat slightly to the side of a bar known as "Cowboy Bill's". I did this work on my own because this is what friends do for one another and by this time I really hoped John was my friend because he sure was a lousy business partner. I would find out otherwise later on but even before K.W.I. was open, my eyes were beginning to see what was really happening with John's idea of loyalty.

I became close to John's sister, Pamela. She came into the picture when John got a crazy idea of opening an eating establishment called "Smokin' Joe's". This was to be a tribute to John's brother who had passed away a couple of years prior. The menu was all smoked dishes and the idea was actually a good one. There wasn't another eating establishment right there in Key West with that type of theme. However, as everyone knows, the key to a successful business is "location, location, location". Well, the location was on Petronia Street off of Duval just a stone's throw away from the 801 Club, a local bar and Drag show club as well as the drug dealing district. The three businesses at the location John had selected had all failed because of that one drawback, the location. In fact, very few businesses off the main drag (Duval) had ever made it big. It was true that having a smoked rib place was a good idea in itself but being so close to the local crack/cocaine district just did not seem to make sense to me. John was supposed to be the big business man. He owned his own stucco business, for God's sake. What was he thinking?

I spent hundreds of hours working on that restaurant with John and even went on a hunt to find a portable smoker. I eventually located one up in the Palm Bay area. John had no idea as to how to run an eating place but he knew someone who did and that was his sister, Pamela. She had spent years in the bar and grill industry in Fort Lauderdale. John called her up one day after not having spoken to her in years. Out of the blue, he just tells her what he has in mind, that he needs someone to run the joint and he promised that it would be very lucrative for her. So she just dropped everything, quitting her job of six years, to come to Key West.

Prior to Pamela's arrival, Smokin' Joe's was running in the red day after day, week after week. But Pamela knew how to run a bar and grill and how to make people feel comfortable. She was one of the most enjoyable people I had been around in a long time and it was actually fun working with her. She seemed to have a knack for drawing people into the restaurant. It wasn't long before the restaurant reversed from red to black. Word was getting around, not only that the place offered up some damned good eats, but that it was a place to have fun. Pamela was very solicitous of the customers and flirted with the men without pissing off their girlfriends or wives. She just had that talent. She was, in my opinion, the sole reason that the restaurant had customers. Without her, there would be no Smokin' Joe's!

Well, like they say, all good things must come to an end
and so that is what happened to Joe's. John got a phone
call from his son, J.B., who had left Key West a couple
of months earlier because he wasn't getting his own way
with things he had suggested to his dad. He had been
working to help open K.W.I., making about $500.00 a
week doing so . . . or should I say *not* doing so. He really
hadn't contributed a damned thing to our tattoo business
but John had paid him a salary just the same. Before leaving
Key West, J.B. had talked his dad into investing about
twenty grand in a Wi-Fi business in Key West. Turned out
that J.B. (and John) had been conned by some guy who
had promised to make both of them rich with the Wi-Fi
deal and the business never opened although the twenty
thousand was gone. Then J.B. skipped town and ended
up in Virginia working for a used car dealer which turned
out to be a losing proposition for him. I myself couldn't
see this kid selling anything except maybe some dope and
I figured the way he operated, he'd end up in the slammer
sooner than later.

So the kid talked his dad into letting him come home
and John gave up the Smokin' Joe's restaurant to his son . . .
kicking Pamela out of the business altogether. As soon as
the son got the key to the place, he headed straight for
the cash register, emptied it, and then looted the safe. He
was married to really nice girl but J.B. decided to divorce
her and go on a spending spree of his own. Yeah, this kid
was a real winner. Daddy John actually paid off J.B.'s wife
(I think it was ten grand) to leave town and she actually
did go. However, it wouldn't be long before she would be
back in J.B.'s life, crying the blues, because she ran out
of money. That is another thing about John: He thinks

money is the answer to everything and that he could buy off anyone for ten or twenty grand.

During Pamela's stay in Key West, she and I got about as close as two people could possibly get. One day, we were catering a small get together at the Key West museum where they were hosting a farewell party for the curator. John was short handed, I had nothing better to do since K.W.I. wasn't officially open yet and I thought maybe I could make a good impression on some of the area's more elite citizens who would be attending. My job was to hand out the beef brisket and so I turned to Pamela and asked her if she would like some beef. Well, the smirk that graced her face was one I don't believe I'll ever forget! After that get together, we had one of our own, if you know what I mean. This had been coming on for some time because I was attracted to her in more ways than one. The affair continued on for several months and sometime during our relationship, Pamela told me a story about the day John's mother had died.

John's mom lived in a little town outside Vero Beach, Florida. She was asking the people who were caring for her to contact her son John in Key West. She couldn't leave the world without seeing her boy. She wanted to make amends before she passed away. When John was contacted, he was sitting in his truck on a construction site and he said, "Fuck the bitch, I got nothin' to say to her!" When Pamela told me this story, I couldn't believe how callous anyone could be, even John, especially to his own mother. It was about this time I really began to worry about this guy I had given over a year of my life to, the thousands of man hours I had spent, not to mention all the money I had invested in K.W.I. I thought to myself that if a man can do something so heinous to his own mother, then where do I stand with him?

There were times when I looked at the tattoo work I had done on John and realized he had them done for all the wrong reasons. He was trying to be someone he wasn't, promoting a business he knew little to nothing about. He was not at all passionate the way I was (and still am) about the business and the art; rather, he concentrated on making money and it did not matter who he had to step on in order to get it. His Pirate tattoos represented old Key West history to him so he had me apply the very best of artistic pirate art on his skin. He wanted to impress the public, represent old Key West. Instead, when I look at him now I see a pirate of sorts in his own eyes. He is the pirate that is inked on his back and arms. I realized suddenly that without me . . . and without the other fine artists I had hired . . . he wouldn't make it in this business. He just didn't have the smarts and he wasn't what one might call "likable". Sooner or later the tourists and residents alike would see his true colors. That would be a sad day for him, but then, I would probably be out of Key West Ink eventually. That is when his real trouble would begin.

One day after an on-going disagreement concerning a number of issues about the management of our new studio, I voiced a concern I had about one of the artists who was working with us. He did not seem to have the same skills he had shown as an airbrush artist. To me it seemed that he had fallen back into some very bad habits he'd had when he first started with us, mainly involving a bag of cocaine with a beer chaser. We also had a female artist named Dixie who proved to have the heaviest hand in the business, rushing to finish one job to get to another and in doing so, not doing the quality work I expected of her. I noticed that there seemed to be a lot of bleeding during Dixie's tattoo applications and that concerned me a lot. She was a self-proclaimed tattoo artist who did not know how to run an autoclave sterilizing machine. That was scary. During the course of three months at K.W.I., I had received numerous complaints over the internet from disgruntled clients who had been in town visiting and had stopped to have a tattoo done. In every case, Dixie was the tattooist. Even some of the locals started complaining. This had me concerned because it would not take much for someone to file a lawsuit against our company for a health hazard inflicted on them.

I tried to bring these items to John's attention but it seemed he already knew all about it and did not want to hear anything I had to say. He wanted to just let matters be as they were, not ruffle any of the artists' feathers. Frustrated, I began to realize that there would be a big change around the studio soon . . . I was almost ready to walk out. However, it had been ninety days and I still had nothing to show for all my efforts and hard work that had gone into opening the most popular tattoo studio in Key West. Every time I questioned John about my shares (the 49% I had been promised), he would skirt around the issue and then just disappear from sight. He was damned good at that.

I had had all that I could take. I knew what kind of man John was and although I was disappointed in him and in myself for being so trusting, I knew I had to do something.

"John, you've had your chance, you've given me the run around every time I try to talk to you about my share of the company, and you're just screwing with me. Enough is enough". He glared at me with hatred steaming out of his eyes. I told him I was going to hire an attorney to come after his ass because this puppy wasn't going to be kicked around anymore.

John was a con artist. How he ever made it as a business man in the stucco business is beyond me. He hid behind the title of "contractor" as he went about his business of using people. Even his wife seemed afraid of him. The way he had treated his own mother, his sister Pamela, and me . . . well, it did not sit well with me. I was fed up once and for all but I had learned a hell of a lesson in the meantime.

I went back to Palm Bay for a few days, needing to gather my thoughts. I knew now that John was going to try to beat me out of my share of the company's holdings when I received an e-mail from him saying my services were no longer needed. I also received an e-mail from a mortgage holder for 717 Duval Street L.L.C. It said that K.W.I. was two months in arrears on the mortgage payments. I couldn't believe what I was reading. How could that possibly be? We had made approximately $70,000.00 in the first ninety days and our overhead was only about $30,000.00. Sounds like someone was having a money management problem and it wasn't me, that was for sure.

John had a co-partner in the ownership of the actual building on Duval. Darrell had what he figured was a great investment with that property. I asked Darrell to meet me for breakfast the next morning and I took along the e-mail with me. I explained the entire situation to Darrell in great detail. I didn't even eat my breakfast, I was so riled up. Darrell appeared calm and collected, but I could tell he was starting to see the inside.

"I'm supposed to be receiving a check every month based on my investment," he told me. That was something strictly between him and John because I wasn't part of the L.L.C. partnership, just in the business end. "I just figured John would catch up with me soon enough and I wasn't too worried. I haven't received any notification from the lien holder that we're past due on the payments,"

So now he was looking at the possibility of a foreclosure because the investor holding the note was leaving the country and had instructed his own attorney to begin foreclosure proceedings. The investor wanted a check in the amount of $18,000.00 or he would immediately act on his threat.

It turned out that Darrell made a few phone calls and squared it away, at least for the meantime. But I could see the writing on the wall. Key West Ink was in big trouble and maybe it was best that I had gotten out when I did.

During the next few months, I continued going to Key West every other weekend. I had made a bunch of friends during my involvement with K.W.I. I also contacted several attorneys concerning my legal rights to ownership in the studio. Two attorneys assured me that I had a great case on my hands, that 49% of the business venture's profits were legally mine because we had made a verbal "gentleman's" agreement regarding this. Florida law considers a verbal agreement as a binding contract. But I had much more than just a verbal agreement based on words passed between John and me and a handshake; I had transcripts, receipts and witnesses as to my standing in K.W.I. I even had a copy of the business plan with my name on it, the same business plan that was brought to Darrell concerning his investment in the K.W.I. building on Duval.

I decided on an attorney in Key West who came highly recommended to me by a couple of locals. He and I met and I explained the whole situation to him. He was mesmerized by the story I told him, again in great detail, and his words were: "This guy is a real piece of work!" Truer words have never been spoken!

My attorney agreed to take on the case but not before I came up with a retainer. I paid him his price and suddenly felt as if the weight was about to tumble off my shoulders. I could sleep a little easier knowing that the ugly mess was in good hands at last. I did not realize how much a good lawyer costs these days. Let's put it this way: $5,000.00 doesn't go very far these days. It was clear to me now the meaning behind something someone once said to me. "Justice, yeah you can get justice providing you can afford it. Other then that, it's **just us**." I always thought I made pretty good money because I average $125.00-$150.00 an hour when I am slinging ink on a regular basis.

It became quite clear that I was going to have to sling a lot more in order to handle my legal issues.

VII

I made some great friends while in Key West, mostly military personnel who were stationed at the local bases. So after I parted ways with K.W.I., (at least for the time being) I was given a chance to work at Sigsbee Navy base in Sigsbee Park. Chief Dockery had a hand in getting me a place there where I could sling ink legititimately. A lot of these enlisted guys had entrusted their skin to me and wore tattoos I had inked on them with pride when I had operated out of Key West Ink.

One day I was introduced to a guy who was called "Mad Man Jake", a real character, funny as hell. He never ran out of stories to tell and what I truly liked about him is that I knew he was telling the truth. His life had been one crazy time after another.

Jake worked with Special Forces in Key West. He worked at the Scuba school ran solely by Special Forces. He was in charge of operations. When he had time off, which was not often, you could find him on his boat fishing or diving in the turquoise and blue waters of Key West. I did some work on Jake's arm, adding to an existing piece he'd had done some time before. The next thing I know, I had a bunch of his comrades in Special Forces coming by to get some work done of their own. The more work I put out, the more work I got. By this time, I had been doing the bi-weekly trip to Key West for about five months and I got a call from Chief Dockery. As it turned out, one of his Special Forces guys I had done some work on, Craig had dropped by Key West Ink showing off the work. It appeared that the work I had been adding to a job done by one of John's less than professional artist's, the guy who was an airbrush artist turned tattooist. It seems I remember Craig, having some work done when I was working at 717 Duval.

Well, I guess the artist got his feelings hurt and the next thing you know John is calling his attorney and told him some lame story about how I was slinging ink on Key West Army and Navy personnel. His attorney wrote a letter to the base commander telling him that I was a "disgruntled ex-employee" who was working on his base as a tattoo artist. Well, I was concerned about this for about a minute or so. Maybe less. You see, I had an ace up my sleeve. John underestimated me this time because I had my ass covered long before John ever turned snitch. Little did John know that the investigation went as far as the nearest file thirteen/circular file. Chief Dockery was my sponsor on base; he was my ticket to do what I was doing legally. It was his place I stayed at while in Key West. I slung mad ink right there in the dining room area, every other week. The Chief's pad was converted into a tattoo parlor on weekends when I was there. I took good care of the guys and they took good care of me. I never charged them but I was tipped handsomely.

Top Gun Pilots, High ranking non-commissioned officers, Special Forces scuba instructors and every rank in between sought out tattoo work from me. I am still the only guy who does skin art on most of the military there. John doesn't like this and neither does his nemesis, Paradise Tattoo. I am and was hurting John in the worst place possible: his pocket. Don't you just love it when Karma really does come around and takes care of things for you? It is the contributions made by the soldiers that have allowed me to handle the sky-rocketing attorney fees involved in this case.

John will not let go easily. He knows he is in the wrong. He has hurt a lot of people, not just me. Greed is an ugly thing and one of these days, he will be the one with the empty pockets because he continues to take advantage of people who work for him as well as the people who become clients of his business.

In the meantime, I am just laying back . . . enjoying my work in Key West when I am there just as I enjoy my work at my own studio here in Palm Bay, Florida. I can't tell you how good it feels to have been able to take my life back and live it to my own accord. I see my family more often, even my twin brother Walter who lives near by. My kids are proud of their dad and I thank God every day that I got away from the crazy man at Key West Ink.

I learned a lot during my trip down the road to Key West Ink. It was one helluva' ride, a bumpy journey, but I now know who I can trust and who I can't. At least I think I know. And I'm happy being trusting, but not naive. Never again will someone pull the wool over this skinny little guy's eyes.

Because I can see straight through that wool for the first time in a very long time. And what I see is that light at the end of the tunnel. I'm not through with this fight, no sir. Like I said before, don't go telling Boe Mencarelli he can't do something; because then it will for sure get done. I am ready to fight, and I will see this through. The Key West Ink that I envisioned is the same tattoo studio that I plan to open in the near future, in my name. The road will still be bumpy. I will probably have to face the powers that be in city council meetings once again. I am not so worried this time, because I know that I have a right to what is legally, lawfully and morally mine. Ain't nothing gonna' stop me now. Onward and upward. In the meantime, I am working hard at Tat2Times Inc., trying to pull in enough business to finance my fight with John and his attorney, if he even has one. This is something I won't give up on. Not in the immediate future. Probably not at all.

And . . . Never give up on your dream. Never let the wool be pulled so tight over your eyes that you can't see the possibilities that lie before you. Because if you do . . . if you do . . . than you will be letting someone else, or something else, control your life and your destiny.

Key West Ink is still in my future.

And that, my friends, is all I am saying right now.

All I am saying.

The End

Epilogue

After many months of haggling with John over the ownership of the business, Boe and his new business partner, Darrell, managed to gain 100% ownership of the business known as Key West Ink. At this writing, he is busy making changes to the business, including a name change, Southernmost Tattoo. His business is still located at 717 Duval Street, a storefront location in the heart of busy Key West. Realizing his dream, Boe never knows what might lay ahead for him . . . another tattoo studio perhaps? One thing is for sure. Life is never boring for Boe Mencarelli.

www.ingramcontent.com/pod-product-compliance
Lightning Source LLC
Chambersburg PA
CBHW022105170526
45157CB00004B/1489